Letters to Mark

Transcripts from Father to Son
Across 3 Countries

Noel W. Davis

BALBOA.
PRESS
A DIVISION OF HAY HOUSE

Balboa Press books may be ordered through booksellers or by contacting:

Balboa Press
A Division of Hay House
1663 Liberty Drive
Bloomington, IN 47403
www.balboapress.com.au
1 (877) 407-4847

Because of the dynamic nature of the Internet, any web addresses or
links contained in this book may have changed since publication and
may no longer be valid. The views expressed in this work are solely those
of the author and do not necessarily reflect the views of the publisher,
and the publisher hereby disclaims any responsibility for them.

The author of this book does not dispense medical advice or prescribe the use
of any technique as a form of treatment for physical, emotional, or medical
problems without the advice of a physician, either directly or indirectly. The
intent of the author is only to offer information of a general nature to help
you in your quest for emotional and spiritual well-being. In the event you use
any of the information in this book for yourself, which is your constitutional
right, the author and the publisher assume no responsibility for your actions.

Print information available on the last page.

ISBN: 978-1-5043-1445-9 (sc)
ISBN: 978-1-5043-1446-6 (e)

Balboa Press rev. date: 08/28/2018

Contents

Appendices

This book is dedicated to Disability Services, Queensland, Ipswich and South West region and more recently to the Department of Communities, Disability Services and Seniors. Particularly to Mark's carers who have worked, and work, in his household.

Letter 1

The Davis family in Fiji, Suva and Nasavusavu.
Mark's birth in Suva.

Dear Mark

As I've aged I am occasionally given to reminiscing so I got to thinking about your life. There is much to tell. I've decided the most interesting way to do so is to write you some letters.

In 1963 your mother, who from now on I'll call Mary, and your two older brothers Paul and Stephen and I were in Fiji. We had gone there with the Overseas Missions Department of the Australian Methodist Church. Paul was about 3 and Stephen 1. We had been in Fiji for nearly a year. I had been given a role in the Rewa Division of the largest island in the group Viti Levu (big Fiji). My most important activity was working at learning to speak and write Fijian. At the Conference of the Methodist Church in Fiji in 1963 I was made Assistant Divisional Superintendent of the Vanua Levu (big land) Division of the church, Vanua Levu being the second largest island of the Fiji group. I was also made principal of the Naqelekula (red soil) Bible School in Nasavusavu where we would live.

This is all background to your beginnings. Mary and I had decided we wanted to have four children and you were to be the third. We thought it would be much easier for you to be born in Suva where there is a major hospital and fully fledged doctors. This took a good deal of planning on our part. You were born on 30th April 1964 and weighed 9lbs 12 ozs. You got a good start. When Stephen was born, Paul felt quite left out of the process so we determined to include both of your brothers this time, This meant when it was time for Mary to go to the hospital, even though it was the middle of the night, we all set off together and I can still remember Paul and Stephen leaning out of the car windows waving to Mary as she stood in the hospital door.

Our move to Nasavusavu was quite a major one. We had to move all our stuff, not that we had a lot of furniture. There were five of us now that you were born. You were just a few weeks old when we moved. A Fijian lady who had started working in the house in Suva moved with us. Her name was Naomi Biturogoiwasa. When we started settling in on our arrival in Fiji we were told that it was usual to have a Fijian lady working in the house. I have to say that we weren't happy about it as it seemed like we had a "servant". She did the housework and prepared the meals. We wanted her to eat with us and managed to persuade her to do so on the first day but when she went home and checked with her parents about the situation she resolutely refused to eat with us in the future. She was a tremendous asset, a lovely person, and able to guide us as we got used to our new surroundings. Our goods and chattels went over to Nasavusavu by ship but we travelled by plane. Fiji Airlines was the local company and they mostly used Herons, a twin engined plane which took 15 passengers. The weight had to be carefully distributed so each person was weighed as well as the luggage. We never got tired of the flights between Suva and. Nasavusavu as they gave us an excellent view of the various islands of the Fiji group and the reefs. Coming into Nasavusavu was always quite hair raising. The plane would go a fair way out to sea over Nasavusavu Bay and then turn towards the strip and as it came in it seemed that the tip of the wing was perilously close to the coconut trees growing on a hillside.

We lived in a large, old style house with a large verandah on two sides. From the front verandah we could look across Nasavusavu Bay, an absolutely beautiful view with the Bay in the foreground and the mountains on the other side in the distance. The house was located on a property of more than 80 acres stretching from the beach to the hills with a little creek running through it. From the back of the house we looked down into a small valley where there were a number of bures (Fijian houses). Some of them were larger than others and accommodated the thirty or so students of the Bible school. There were a couple of staff living on the property. One was a Vakatawa, a Home Missionary, who helped in the Bible School and accompanied me when I visited the churches in various parts of Vanua Levu. We made a pact early in the piece that we would not use English, even though he was quite proficient, unless there was an emergency, otherwise he would help me struggle to express myself in Fijian. There was also a young Rabean minister who taught in the Bible school. Paul started to go to a Part European school when he was five where the classes were in English and Stephen gradually became acquainted with some of the children around and became quite adept at expressing himself in Fijian. They both enjoyed running around the property and were popular with the students.

All that gives the background to the next major event in your life, a rather tragic one for you and indeed for everyone but I will get onto that in the next letter.

Love Dad.

Letter 2

*Mark comes down with meningitis. Treatment in
Nasavusavu and Suva. Mark's eventual return to
Australia with grandmother and grandfather.*

Dear Mark,

We had only been in Nasavusavu for about three months
when you became quite ill. You started with a heavy cold
which seemed to develop into the flu. We took you to the
local hospital which was in easy walking distance of our
house. The hospital was staffed by an Indian Medical Orderly,
well trained but not a Doctor. He administered antibiotics
but the illness continued to take its course and it seemed to
develop into pneumonia and you were getting worse. The
next morning Mary took you up to the hospital as we were
very worried about your worsening condition. The Medical
Orderly only had to hear the cry that you had developed to
suspect that you had meningitis. We learnt later that there
is a unique cry which children with meningitis use. He said
that you had to go to Suva for treatment as soon as possible.
You stayed in hospital where your temperature was so high
the nurses sponged you off constantly and a fan was trained
directly on to you. While we had heard of meningitis we didn't
know exactly what it was or its effects. When we consulted
the Encyclopedia Britannica we were not encouraged. We
discovered that it is caused by an infection which gets into the
meninges, the tissues around the brain and that it can cause
brain damage and even death.

We called the airport office and booked you and Mary on the morning plane. The weather was bad and it was extremely doubtful that the plane would be able to land but the pilot knew it was an emergency. We waited by the phone ready to leave for the airport immediately. There was a break in the cloud cover and we got the phone call so that you headed for Suva with Mary. An ambulance met you both at Suva airport and took you to hospital. The diagnosis of the Medical Orderly was confirmed and treatment started. You were in hospital for two weeks during which time Mary stayed with the Robsons who were also Missionaries living in Suva.

Over the years we have learned from people who had been affected with meningitis and had obviously recovered that the pain is intense. We have only been able to imagine it but your head went back in an effort to relieve the pain. The major test for the condition is a spinal tap and in your case some fluid was taken through the fontanelle, the last part of the skull to develop and still soft in a baby. Your life was in the balance and to say it was an anxious time would be an understatement. I can remember kneeling in prayer on the verandah of the house in Nasavusavu. I had been reading a number of books by Glenn Clark, the founder of the Camp Farthest Out movement. I think it was in one of these that I read of the following approach which I am no longer sure about, but it was desperation time. In these circumstances when faced with the serious illness of a loved one, it was suggested that one, in effect, let them go, sort of give them and their recovery over to God. I can remember endeavouring to do this and not being sure if I had been able to do so. At the time of your illness there were a great many people in Fiji and Australia praying for you. Some would say that the prayers were answered in that you lived and, of course, I am very grateful but there's a lot more to be said and I will be coming back to this in a later letter.

It was a tremendous struggle for you to overcome the illness with the aid of antibiotics and many people who are affected with the particular strain of virus which afflicted you, the pneumococcyl, do not survive. After a couple of weeks you came out of hospital and back to our home in Nasavusavu. Mary had noticed changes in your responses even in hospital and these became more and more obvious. You had largely lost your desire to feed and it would take one and a half hours to give you a bottle. You were not as alert as before and you blanked out periodically and seemed to go into spasm, eyes rolling and with some shaking. We were completely unfamiliar with epileptic seizures but that was what you were having. We got in touch with the hospital in Suva and eventually Mary took you back. We have never been able to understand the attitude of the Doctor who was treating you. I see no point in mentioning his name. He stated that they were unable to observe the seizure activity and suggested to Mary that she had a normal child and should treat you as such. You were definitely having seizures and we have learned that there is even a term, post-meningeal epilepsy to cover this situation. Also, they were very familiar with the treatment of meningitis as it is very common in Fiji. At that stage nobody seemed to know why it is so prevalent. With the great number of mosquitos in various part of Fiji, it would seem to follow that the disease is mosquito born but at that time this was not generally accepted.

When it came time for Mary to bring you home Fiji was on the edge of a cyclone. There were strong winds and the weather was generally uncertain. The plane left Suva but it wasn't known whether it would be able to land in Nasavusavu. I went to the airport, that sounds a little exaggerated – it was an airstrip with a small shelter shed and office. When the plane arrived, the pilot tried to come in over the sea, rather than over the bay as usual but the wind was too strong. He then went to try from the usual direction. As we waited we could see the plane coming down past the hills I mentioned earlier but as it came in ready to land the wind took it and it seemed to slip towards the shelter shed. We all ran as it looked like it would hit the shed. At the last minute the pilot pulled out of the landing and went round for a third attempt before finally heading back to Suva. You can imagine what it was like for Mary in the plane as it moved round alarmingly and she clutched on to you. It was the next day when the weather had settled that you came home.

On your return home things basically continued as before with you not really wanting to eat. The centre in your brain which governs appetite had been damaged. This meant feeding was a constant problem and a long drawn out procedure. Mary or Naomi would anchor your arm down and just persist till they felt you had taken in enough milk which often had an egg mixed with it and gradually added solid food. The next major event which had a direct bearing on you was the arrival of your grandmother on Mary's side and your step grandfather, Cec. Buckle. They had been in New Zealand for the marriage of Cec's older son and then came up to visit us. We had just been through a cyclone. Fortunately we were not in its direct path but it was scary enough with winds of over 100 kilometres an hour which uprooted a few coconut palms near the house. Your grandmother and Cec. were very disturbed when they saw your condition and offered to take you back to Australia to be checked out by doctors in Brisbane. When all the preparations were made you headed off. Mary didn't go at that stage as we didn't have enough money for the airfare and the Mission Board was not prepared to pay for her travel. We heard later that you didn't travel well and that your grandparents were very concerned about you.

A number of tests were done on you in Brisbane and you were under the main care of Dr. Felix Arden. They did a brain x-ray and electro-encephalograms which became very common with you over the years. The x-ray was the particularly telling procedure and we received a letter from your grandmother giving us the grim news. We read that you had sustained two thirds brain damage. We both sat on the bed and howled. I guess till then we had hoped that there would be some degree of recovery or maybe the full extent of your illness and its possible effects had not hit us. At that moment it was the sense of loss that gripped us. You were a beautiful, healthy baby with all the promise that has been realised in your older brothers and now you were intellectually handicapped. I'm not sure we have ever come to terms with it even though as you developed and grew we dealt with the various situations as best we could.

It's a sad way to finish this letter but there's a lot more to be covered in future letters because you had a great impact on the way our lives developed.

Love Dad

Letter 3

Mary goes back to Australia and her return to the USA.
The decision to go to get special treatment for Mark.
Noel is appointed to a church in San Diego.

Dear Mark,

In the last letter I mentioned the tests administered in Brisbane and the extent of the brain damage you had sustained. When we let the Mission Board know they agreed to pay for Mary to fly back to Australia to be with you. I had planned to visit some villages on the other side of Nasavusavu Bay with the aim of being back well before she had to leave. The major part of my work was to keep in touch with the ministers and their congregations and to endeavour to give encouragement and support. The trip across the bay got quite hairy as in one part there was no reef so the waves rolled straight in from the open sea. On the way back we had to get our boat towed by a launch as both outboard motors we had with us had packed up. We managed to get home on the evening before Mary left for Australia.

Your grandmother, Eizzil Buckle had taken you from hospital to their home in Buderim. Mary was met at the plane by your paternal grandfather, Vic Davis and taken to Buderim where you were reunited with Mary. The two of you also spent some time with the Davis grandparents and you had your first birthday there and sat up. Meanwhile back in Nasavusavu Naomi helped look after Paul and Stephen so I was able to continue with my work. One of the main things which was worked out with the Doctors in Brisbane was a balance of drugs to control your epilepsy. As I mentioned in the note on epilepsy (see Appendix 1) this has been an ongoing process. As you got older other drugs were prescribed for hyperactivity. Sometimes through a build up of drugs you would become ataxic and drowsy. It was a matter of finding a balance which controls epilepsy and hyperactivity but still allows you to function to your potential.

It was great to have Mary and you back home. Life proceeded but great effort was needed to encourage and most times force you to eat. People from America used to send magazines to Fiji to be distributed as church staff saw fit. In a more current Reader's Digest Mary came across an article about a method of treating people who had suffered brain damage. For some reason I can recall being in the car parked near the village called Yaroi which was at the foot of the hill on which Naqelekula is located. Mary and I both read it and became excited as I guess we hadn't lost hope that somehow your condition could be treated so that you could develop to be at least closer to what you could have been. The method was named after the two people who had come up with it – Doman- Delecato. Their theory was that when brain cells are damaged other cells can be retrained to take over their function. The re-training is done mainly through a process of taking the individual back through regular patterns of creeping and crawling. The second Appendix gives a more detailed description of the method. They were located in Philadelphia and we wrote to the address given. We eventually received a reply saying that a new facility had been opened in San Diego and they suggested we contact them. We did that and were informed that if we could get to San Diego you would be assessed and treatment prescribed. We were at that stage in the third year of our appointment with the Board of Missions, due to go home on furlough at the end of four years. We had a major decision to make, would we finish our term and go back to Australia and get the best treatment we could there, or venture to America. We decided on the latter and approached the Mission Board to ask them if they would provide the money which they would have paid to get us home on furlough towards our trip. They agreed. In the back of my mind I had the thought that at some stage in America I would have the chance to do more study.

An important consideration was supporting ourselves in the US. I wrote to the Bishop of the United Methodist Church in whose diocese San Diego was located explaining what we were hoping to do and asking if there was an appointment in the area which I could fill. They must have encouraged us to proceed with our plans but I seem to recall that we didn't hear of the actual appointment until close to the time we boarded the ship to the USA. I was to be the Associate Pastor at Pacific Beach United Methodist Church in San Diego. As things were falling into place we had to finish off our work in Fiji.

That's probably more than enough for one letter so will close.

Love Dad

Letter 4

Leaving Fiji on the ship "Arcadia". Difficulties having Mark accepted by American Immigration. The passage and ports of call.

Dear Mark,

Our decision to leave Fiji had been made rather quickly so farewells were not prolonged and we proceeded to pack up. As seems to have always happened when we have moved we ran out of packing space and I had to purchase at least one more suitcase from the local general store run by a Chinese merchant. It intrigued me that when visiting various villages miles and miles off the beaten track one would sometimes come across a store which carried almost everything that anyone could want, run invariably by a Chinese merchant. The Chinese in Fiji often intermarried with native Fijians and the children of these marriages were particularly beautiful. At the time we were in Fiji there was no intermarriage between the native Fijians and the Indians who had been brought into the country to work the cane fields. On a much more recent trip we discovered that these racial groups had, at least started, to intermarry. We were sad to leave the people of Nasavusavu, particularly those at Naqelekula where our house and Bible school were. I had bought a horse which we named Peter from someone who lived locally as I was thinking of riding to nearby villages but didn't ever follow through on the idea. I gave the horse to Tikilaci Vocea as I was particularly grateful for his help on the various "raicakacaka", (trips looking at the work). I enjoyed his company and guidance.

In Suva we stayed with the Robsons and again were glad of their generous hospitality. John Nix was the accountant for the church in Fiji, appointed by the Mission Board. He and Betty and their family had been in Fiji for some years. I had brought the Vanua Levu Division books back from Nasavusavu which John checked and got in order. Given the financial problems the Division had, it was a source of enormous satisfaction to me to learn that the skimping on travel costs had paid off and the account was in the black.

We had booked on the Arcadia and had arranged passages and passports for all of us. To get an American visa those over 6 years had to have blood tests. I was amazed how much blood they took. One of the tests was for venereal disease, a sexually transmitted disease. It intrigued Mary and I that Paul was also given this test. Not long before we were due to leave, the American Consul in Fiji discovered that you had sustained brain damage through meningitis and were therefore physically and mentally disabled. To our horror we learned that, in American immigration law there is a clause which excludes disabled people whose condition starts at some stage after birth. We have never been sure why this information had not been recognised till then. The verdict was that Mary, yourself and your brothers may have to wait for a clearance and then perhaps fly over and join me. I think we knew that this would never happen. The Fijian consul tried to contact the consul in Honolulu, the point of entry for those travelling to the USA. It was a very anxious time and I remember pacing the floor in the Consul's office. I think this happened on the week end and the consul in Hawaii could not be contacted so that the decision was made that we would travel to Honolulu where the matter would be reviewed – a massive relief. We were also very grateful to Naomi who had lived with us for almost the whole of the time in Fiji and we had a great deal of affection for her. She had shown particular care for you after your contracting of meningitis but really of the whole family. On the two occasions Mary and I have been back to Fiji we have tried to meet up with her. We met up with her in Centenary, the huge church in Suva which seats about 1000 people, and we had lunch together. On the second occasion, in 2015, we were saddened to learn that she had died.

When the time came for us to board ship it was with very mixed feelings. There were the expectations of a new venture, but also a great sadness to be leaving Fiji, which we had come to love, and the friends we had made. There are some clear memories as we left the wharf. It was the custom at the time for one of the two top class bands in Fiji, one drawn from the Police Force and the other from the military to play as the ship left, also as ships arrived. On leaving, the major piece played was Isa Lei. A farewell lament, guaranteed to bring tears to the eyes. Among those who came to see us off were Naomi and Marge Bollen, now Marge Bonser who had been in All Saints Missionary College in Sydney with us for six months and visited us in Nasavusavu. She was and is a lovely person. As we pulled away from the wharf and stood at the rail of the ship one of the last things we could see of people standing there was Marge who was holding an umbrella against the powerful tropical sun moving her umbrella up and down to wave goodbye. As we left, our affection for the place and people was such that we thought that we would eventually resume our work there, but this was not to be.

We discovered that there was a play room for children on the ship where we spent a great deal of time on the voyage. Paul and Stephen enjoyed it. You also spent time there but Mary or I had to be present the whole time as your hyperactivity meant that you could well wander off. We think Mary and I ate meals at the same time as Paul and Stephen, children had their meals earlier than everyone else, and that you had your meals brought to the cabin so we could feed you there. A lady who worked in the play room offered to come and look after you while the rest of us had our meals. While we were in Nasavusavu I had been approached by the Scout Commissioner in Fiji about becoming District Commissioner for the area. I had never been involved in Scouts as a boy but I agreed as it seemed to complement my work. This meant there was a Scout Commissioner who hadn't even got through his "tenderfoot", the first step in scouting. The reason I mention this is that on board ship we discovered that because of my involvement with scouting I was on a V.I.P. list, which is made up covering passengers who board at each port en route. This meant we were invited to a special reception to meet the Captain and were contacted by the seafood chef who was a member of the Deep Sea Scouts who, for whatever reason, travel a lot and are able to contact a network of people in various places throughout the world. Both Mary and I love seafood and on two occasions he brought a selection of food to our cabin so we felt privileged and duly indulged ourselves.

The other highlights of the trip involved berthing at ports en route. The first was at Pago Pago in American Samoa. Passengers could book on various trips ahead of time. Sitting for any length of time was a definite problem for you but we found it wasn't too much more expensive to ask a taxi driver to take us round the major attractions. We discovered that American Samoa shares a similar beauty to

Fiji, being volcanic in origin and tropical. We followed the same arrangement in Honolulu with the taxi but managed to spend extra time at Waikiki, the famous beach where we had a swim.

The water was beautifully warm but we felt the beach was vastly over-rated with coarse sand and a lot of rocks, compared with the beautiful white, sandy beaches along the coast of Australia. The other major entertainment was a visit to Shriner's three ring circus at night. I think we must have asked the lady mentioned earlier to look after you but Paul and Stephen had a great night out. I should add that we couldn't go ashore till some time after everyone else as we had to meet with immigration officers. Honolulu being the point of entry to the USA from the West, your status had to be considered. Even though there is a clause in US immigration law prohibiting the entry of anyone who had become disabled after birth, they decided that we could proceed on the journey but would need to go to the immigration centre at San Ysidro near the Mexican border for a final decision. The only other port of call was Vancouver in Canada. As we approached it in the early morning we ran into thick fog, something which is apparently common in this area. This meant that the fog doors were closed to prepare for possible emergency, and the usual route to the dining room was changed. Paul and Stephen showed how familiar they had become with the ship and a great deal of initiative in going ahead to have breakfast and getting there a long time before you and Mary and myself. We also enjoyed looking round Vancouver. The next port of call was Los Angeles where we were to disembark. Since when we got there we had reached mainland United States and the start of that phase of our lives, I think I'll finish here and continue in the next letter.

Love Dad

Letter 5

Some thoughts about Mark being afflicted with meningitis
and some misunderstandings by well meaning people.

Dear Mark,

Since in the last letter we had entered another phase of our lives with our arrival in America this is probably a good time to talk in a general way about your being afflicted with meningitis and its effects on you. I don't think I mentioned earlier that medical opinion suggested that no matter how long you lived you would not develop mentally, emotionally beyond the processes of a two year old. The opinion was also expressed that you would suffer from a lot of chest complaints and would not survive beyond your teen years. They certainly got that wrong. As I write this you are 52 years old and get fewer colds than the rest of us, although over the years you have had two bouts of pneumonia.

When something so drastic happens to someone or their loved ones it is inescapable to ask, why should this happen to me or us, and we have asked such questions over the years. Of course there is the basic reply that it happened because you were infected with a particular type of meningitis but that doesn't answer the much broader question – why in the general scheme of things. Anyone with a religious faith particularly in the Jewish or Christian tradition, is concerned to do God's will, and feels there is a purpose in all things. So when an event such as this occurs the simple answer is that this is God's will, but to me such an answer is far too simple. Does this mean that

God wants someone, in this case you, to have your potential in life greatly reduced and to be affected with epilepsy and hyperactivity? This doesn't really tie in with a God who is love. Some would say that such events are not brought about by God but by the power of evil and that all that is harmful is the result of a personal devil. This is an attempt at an easy answer but takes away from the overall power of God, and still doesn't answer the question why such a thing should happen to you. People with faith have wrestled with these problems and we have come across a number over the years who have considered that there are answers. Some have suggested that conditions such as yours are a mistake in the overall scheme of things, and that since Jesus healed people then spiritual or faith healing is an option. You have therefore been prayed over and had hands laid on you. Obviously healing did not occur, and such healing, where there is actual damage to an organ, in your case, the brain, rarely if ever occurs. It has even been inferred that epilepsy is brought on by demon possession and that this demon can be cast out. There is an incident recorded in the Gospels in the Bible which suggests that epilepsy may be cured in this way. Basically, this was a first century attempt to explain the condition and did not have the benefit of modern medical science. We took great exception to the suggestion that you might be possessed by a demon. Whatever one's thoughts or approach, for the benefit of all concerned, the point has to be reached where the question is consciously or unconsciously asked, how can I deal with this? In other words there is acceptance of what has happened and then the effort is made to adapt to it in the best way possible. You see, we have sometimes asked would this have happened to you if we hadn't gone to Fiji to serve the church there? Meningitis is far more prevalent in Fiji than Australia. There is no possibility of a clear answer. You may not have been affected with meningitis but had something just as drastic happen. Certainly feeling guilty about what has happened does not in any way help deal with it, indeed it may take away from the coping process. A good illustration of the adapting process is shown I think in what Mary has observed that since you had a mental age of a two year old there were times when you had to be carried, much, much later than other children. As you grew in size and weight so it seemed her physical strength grew, and I would say her emotional strength as well and that of the family. I may not feel guilty about what happened to you as a result of the decision to go to Fiji, and I may have reached acceptance, but that doesn't remove the great sadness that this has happened to you, and the occasional recurring thought of what you could have been. Let me quickly add that you are Mark Walter Davis, that you are alive in the here and now and that we love you.

There's just one other statement that people have made to us occasionally over the years that I want to comment on. It is well meant but still not very helpful. It's been made by someone who has observed us as a family. "God only chooses special families to give someone who is disabled to, so they can cope." Those may not be the exact words but that is the sentiment. When we've heard them we've usually smiled and been pleasant in response while thinking that we could have done without what has happened, first of all because of your condition, and secondly the effects on the family, and I do want to mention those in another letter. The statement implies that we just automatically coped, that somehow we were prepared for it. Incidents in which a family member becomes severely disabled can cause families to fall apart as severe pressure is put on the various relationships. It is natural and I believe inescapable that there is more of a focus on the disabled person. You had to claim more attention which means that in spite of the best intentions, and more of this later, the rest of the family misses out in some way. I believe that this is particularly the case with a mother. There is in most cases a particular bond with the mother and her children which is natural and strong just from having the child develop inside her for 9 months. I know these days there is every opportunity for fathers to develop some sort of bond from the time the baby comes into the world by being at the birth. I wasn't allowed to be present at your birth, or that of Paul and Stephen. Usually a fairly large nursing sister just looked hard at me when we arrived at the hospital suggesting I take off and get out of the road. I have to say, not being made of stern stuff that I was happy not to be there, and Mary has made the comment that she had enough to do giving birth to a baby without having to worry about me as well.

I believe an even more special bond is formed, in many cases, when for some reason one of her children becomes disabled in some way. A mother, of necessity, becomes even more focussed on the well being of that child. Mary has been no exception with you. She hasn't neglected Paul and Stephen or me but has been fiercely protective of you and your well being.

All that is to indicate some of the pressure put on families in these circumstances, and why it is by no means automatic that a family stays together. Also to suggest that somehow God chooses families who are to care for disabled children is to make God very calculating and rather unconcerned about the well being of the person who becomes disabled. Even though people who have made this statement are well meaning we haven't found it very helpful. It really amounts to another attempt to explain how God allows things to happen if one believes that God is responsible for all things.

That is probably more than enough for one letter. I'll get back to the story of our travels but there is a lot to be covered yet on the effects both positive and negative of your becoming disabled. I'll sign off for now.

Love Dad

Letter 6

*Arriving in America at Los Angeles. Settling into
our new home. The generosity of American people.
We're awarded "Immigrant status".*

In the last letter I did some musing, if you like, about your
becoming disabled, and some attempts to explain it and fit
it into the general scheme of things. There'll probably have
to be more of that in later letters as pain and loss are hard to
come to terms with. In the letter before that we had reached
Los Angeles in our travels. There was real excitement as we
moved down the West coast of the US and came into Los
Angeles harbour, a sense of anticipation and more than a
little apprehension about how things would work out. We had
been told that someone from Pacific Beach United Methodist
Church would meet us to take us to San Diego. When we had
cleared customs we were met by Bill and Marte Chamness
and began to discover the warmth and generosity of the large
majority of the American people. Bill seemed a little older than
Marte and was in business in some way. Marte had a PhD in,
I think, Sociology, and we found her to be tremendously
creative and energetic. They took us to the house where we
would spend the next three years right next to the church.
The Senior Minister, Milton Weisshaar and his family lived a
few blocks away from the church. They were rather apologetic
about the house but compared to the parsonage in Oakey on
the Darling Downs where Mary and I started our married
life, and the mission house in Nasavusavu, it was almost a
mansion. Another memory of our first day in Pacific Beach is

of being taken by Milton to a drug store or super market to get a few necessities and standing in the middle of it in total awe at its size and the variety of goods available. We'd just come from two years in Nasavusavu which had a few general stores and a population of maybe 2000 – everything one wanted would be on the next boat.

I learned what my work as an Associate Pastor involved. I would be the "Minister of Evangelism". In this role my main task was to visit new people who came to the church and endeavour to include them in the congregation. I was also to be minister of Youth and be responsible for youth groups in the church. Part of my stipend was being met by Wesley Palms Retirement Home so that part of my role involved being part time Chaplain to the home. This was a rather wealthy establishment and I wondered how I would get on with the residents. I found them very welcoming and they had a very active "religious activities" committee.

Pacific Beach was a beautiful place to live. In climate it is rather similar to Perth, fairly dry and equable in temperature and is situated between the Pacific Ocean on the West and Mission Bay in the East. As part of San Diego it is in Southern California and therefore close to Mexico. There was a lot of settling in for us to do but this was made easier by the warmth and openness of the people we met. Americans in general seem to have an affinity with Australians but had great fun with our accent which we were determined to maintain. At that stage we had no idea how long we would stay. We were there to get treatment for you and had a vague idea of staying for three or four years but finished up being in America for 8 years. While wishing to retain our accent there were some words we had to say differently to be understood, particularly Davis. When we said our name in Australian the Americans would think we were saying Doivis so it had to be a rather snobby longer "a" sound. If we didn't do this when giving our name it would be written down as Divis and it was particularly amusing to the person concerned if we spelt it out and said "a for apple" as they thought we were saying "I for apple". Paul and Stephen, having a good section of their growing up in America have retained some of the accent, though Mary and I don't notice it. It was interesting that as we grew accustomed to hearing the American accent we could detect no difference between that and our own, until we had a visit from an Australian when the difference became very obvious. Stephen had a particularly interesting accent for a while. I remember one day in Fiji hearing two Fijian boys talking as they played and looking out the window to see that one of those boys was Stephen. He can't remember any Fijian but I was envious at the time of his lack of accent. When we moved to America, for Stephen, the Fijian accent became overlaid with that of America.

The almost overwhelming generosity of the American people and the Pacific Beach congregation in particular was shown on our first Sunday. We were given a great welcome in the service but they had declared it a "larder" day and everyone was encouraged to bring something towards setting up a new home. A set of shelves on wheels was set up in the entrance of the church and the people put their gifts there as they came in. We finished up with boxes of goods. It was as overwhelming as it was unexpected, but set the pattern for our experience of the generosity of the average American.

Early in our stay in San Diego we had an appointment with what was called," The Institute for the Achievment of

Human Potential" which was the branch of the organisation in America which practiced the Doman-Delacato method (more information in Appendix 2). We had to give them your history and they ran the first of many EEG's (electro encephalogram). This involved attaching sensors to various part of your head with some sort of "goo". Since you have never liked things on your head and sitting or lying still has never been a strong point, the EEG was more than a little difficult. We learned for the first time that the Institute didn't really work with anyone who had more than 50% brain damage but since we had come from Fiji they would see how things worked out.

They then set a whole lot of routines to be done. The major part of the programme involved patterning which was designed to take you back to creeping. You were placed flat on your stomach on a table with people placed, one at your head, one at each arm and one on each leg, at least ideally. Then, in co-ordinated fashion, your head was turned, an arm and a leg on one side bent up and so on. This was done four times a day, 6 and 10 am, 2 and 6 pm for a few minutes each time. While this was going on whoever was there would count or repeat nursery rhymes. Ever since then you have loved to count, and expected someone to count with you and fill in the gaps, and have remembered a number of nursery rhymes, again enjoying someone filling in missing words. You haven't ever however associated the numbers with anything as e.g. 5 fingers. When the people of Pacific Beach United learned of the need for patterning, some 32 signed to come in at the 10am and 2pm times. The family mainly did the others with Paul at the head and Mary and I on each side. This is an indication of how much Paul and Stephen have been involved very directly in your care and development and I'll be saying more about that later. There was one person, a university student at the time,

Pam Faurote who came in faithfully at 6 am each day. We obviously became very close to her and have kept in touch over the years. The number of people who were prepared to help really impressed us

I should mention a couple of families who particularly stand out in my memory. The first is Pat and Frank Sabatka and their daughter, Toni. They were, you could say, kindred spirits. Toni had undergone surgery to remove a tumour behind one of her eyes. The operation was successful in that she had no further problems with cancer but she sustained some brain damage and, of course, was fitted with an artificial eye. Pat and Frank were particularly helpful with your care. Frank who happened to be off work at the time offered to help me learn to drive in America, since one drives on a different side of the car and road. He also helped me choose a second hand vehicle. I seem to remember a Toyota station wagon. It's just as well he came with me for a while until I got accustomed to the changes. There were a couple of times I wanted to head off on the wrong side of the road. It is when one turns a corner that is particularly awkward and it is easy to go back to what is familiar. We had the same trouble when we eventually returned to Australia, as we had become accustomed to driving in America. As I write this, I'm sad to say Pat, Frank and Toni have all died.

The other person who was particularly helpful was Mary Webster. She had a family of 5 boys and was involved in all sorts of church and community activities and with the patterning, but said to Mary she would look after you for a whole day a month. On that day Mary could do whatever she wanted. If she wanted to go out you would be at home but otherwise she would take you to her place. Mary has never forgotten this as it gave her a break. Another lady who was extremely helpful and fitted in, ready to do whatever was necessary without waiting to be asked was Dottie Heil. With no intention on your part, your care was ongoing and constant, and far more demanding than that of Paul and Stephen ever was. There is a lot more to tell but will save it for the next letters.

Love,
Dad

Letter 7

Other activities with Doman-Delacato programme.
Toilet training. Monosyllables in speech. Family
trip around Western US National Parks.

I'm continuing on from the last letter about life in San Diego. In addition to the patterning part of the Doman-Delacato programme there were a whole lot of other activities which Mary did with you designed to stimulate responses. She made up some pieces of material with a buttonhole and large button sewn on it and encouraged you to do the button up. You have never really learned that skill so that as we tried to teach you to dress yourself we have used shirts which can be pulled over your head and trousers with elastic in the top which can be pulled up. This means that you still need a lot of assistance in dressing, however undressing yourself has never been as difficult and more about that later. We pasted large pictures of animals on to thin plywood and these were held up to you, the animal named and the sounds made. Since we've had a dog in each place we've lived, the "woof, woof" sound is one that you made but as you have become older you no longer do this. You never connected the sound to a dog. You had started to walk in Fiji and soon after to run and climb and could make rapid progress in any direction you started on, but not really with any purpose. It always seemed that you would run in a particular direction till some obstacle – wall, fence etc. got in your way and then you would head left or right. This meant that over the years we had to keep doors locked with special catches, mainly to remind us that the doors or gates needed to be secured. You have over the years made some amazing escape runs and I will write about these when speaking about the places in which we have lived, but it really started in Pacific Beach. There was one occasion when the church custodian, Charlie Cumpston, a fairly elderly gentleman with a love of philosophising, found you stark naked around the church grounds and brought you home. You see, you could take clothes off even though you had a great deal of trouble putting them on. On another occasion you were found crawling across the main road which went past the church, Ingraham Street. This was a very busy road so that it was very fortunate you were not hit by a car. Even though you could walk and run, I have to say, the latter in a fairly uncoordinated way, the program you were on was designed to take you back to creeping and crawling so that you needed to be discouraged from walking. I can't remember all the methods but one stands out in my memory. We bought a pair of roller skates, removed the front wheels and then attached some pieces of broomstick under them. This meant that if you wanted to walk you would have to balance almost on tiptoes, and you managed it. We were never successful in discouraging you from walking, and you showed great determination and ingenuity in overcoming all the efforts made.

Your sensitivity to pain had been blunted through the brain damage that you sustained, so that one day Mary went into the kitchen to find that you were lying across the door of the oven, which was on. Fortunately you were wearing a nappy and that plus the other clothes you were wearing had prevented all but one hand from being burnt.

It was a real milestone in your development when you became toilet trained and this happened at Pacific Beach. It was a result of Mary's persistence. She would leave you without a nappy and as soon as you looked like going to the toilet would rush in and put you on the toilet seat and eventually you made the connection. It is not very common for someone with the extent of brain damage you have to be toilet trained. One day you were saying "toy" and Mary thought you wanted to play with something, and looked around to see what you wanted. However you started to wet and she realised that you meant the toilet. Until today you still say "toy" when you need to go to the toilet, but many times it is a false alarm as you learned that this is also an attention getter or boredom reliever. Whether you are taken to the toilet or not when you use this expression, depends on how recently you have been. As you got older you took yourself to the toilet but were only able to do so when wearing pants with elastic in the top.

It was at this time when you were three or four years old that you started to use quite a few monosyllables as "toy" for toilet and this has been the extent of your speech over the years. You say Mum, Da with a long "a" sound for dad, Poor for Paul, Stea for Stephen. There are a number of others and this has been great. You started to use the word "more" for water when you wanted a drink. We think this happened when you had drunk a glass of water on one occasion and we asked you if you wanted some more. You associated the drink of water with "more" and we have not been able to change this in your mind for over 40 years. You have needed to drink a lot of water over the years as some of the drugs you have taken have made you thirsty. There have been times when we have left a glass near the kitchen tap so that you could get a drink whenever you wanted it, but this had to be done with some care as you didn't distinguish between the hot and cold taps.

When we came due for holidays we decided to take off in our car to some of the National Parks in California and neighbouring states. We have always felt that, apart from particular features, when you have seen one modern city you have seen the lot, but this is not true of natural features. At some stage we traded in the Toyota station wagon for a huge Ford V8 station wagon. I'm not exactly sure why we did this. Perhaps we had in mind the need for more room for camping, because that's what we decided we would have to do if we wanted to be able to afford to travel. We bought a large tent which served us very well over the years and everything else we would need for camping such as a Coleman stove, sleeping bags, air mattresses. It was quite a load. We were on the road for about a month and covered some 7000 miles. Other than trouble with burnt out brakes at one stage, we had a great time. We kept up the patterning quite faithfully, using picnic tables when we stopped for lunch or where we were camping. We visited Sequoia and Yosemite National Parks which we thought were beautiful. It must've been in Sequoia that we were camping near a small stream running over rocks where Paul and Stephen had great fun sliding down on their rear ends, so much so that I think it was Paul who wore a hole in his bathers. We were some of the last people to go through the tunnel in a huge redwood tree. A few years later it came down in heavy snow. We then went up as far as the Canadian border near Vancouver. We were not able to cross over as you would not have been permitted back into the country. We went across to Glacier National Park which also straddled the border and then down to Yellowstone. We went to the northern part of the Grand Canyon and to Bryce and Zion. It was all magnificent country and we feel privileged to have seen it all.

Early in our stay in San Diego we went to the immigration offices in San Ysidro on the Mexican border to check on your status. As I said earlier, technically we should not have been able to bring you into the country. The rest of us had "immigrant status" so that I had a selective service card, and except for my age could have been called up for military service. Since you had been admitted to America the decision was made not to deport you but once you left the country you would not be permitted to return. So, in effect, you were on parole.

That's probably enough for now but there's quite a lot more to write about happenings in San Diego.

Love Dad

Letter 8

More about life in San Diego. Checks on progress at Institute in San Diego. Trip to Philadelphia by Mary and Mark.

Dear Mark,

A bit more about life in San Diego. It was a good three years we had there as a family. Paul and Stephen went to Crown Point elementary school and seemed to fit in very well. Paul joined the Cub Scouts and started to have tennis lessons. We had quite a scare with Stephen one afternoon. He and Paul had gone to a friend's place and were on their way home. They were about to cross the road and came out between a couple of parked cars so that they didn't have good visibility. Paul got across all right but Stephen was hit by a car. Fortunately the driver having seen Paul must have been slowing down. I don't think there was any outward sign of injury but some days later Stephen blanked out, indicating a form of epilepsy and therefore minimal brain damage. You can see why we had a scare, as you had quite massive brain damage and epilepsy. He was put on a mild dose of Dilantin for a while but has never had any more seizures.

There were regular checks on your progress at the Institute in San Diego. It was discovered through the EEGs that you were having sub-clinical seizures. These were not obvious outwardly. The grand-mal seizures were and still are obvious although the seizure activity is mostly under control through combinations of drugs. The Institute were concerned about the subclinical seizure activity and suggested that you be taken to

Philadelphia and examined by Dr Eugene Spitz, a neurologist who worked closely with the Doman-Delacato Program. He with another doctor has given his name to a shunt inserted in the brain to drain away the fluid in cases of hydrocephalus, "water on the brain". When people in the Pacific Beach Church heard about the recommendation to go to Philadelphia two women in the Wesley Palms retirement home who happened to be sisters and attended the church, very kindly offered to pay for the airfare across the states for you and Mary. It was indeed a very generous gift and again an indication of the kindness with which we were treated in our time in America. We think you stayed in Philadelphia for about two weeks. You were in hospital for a time and Mary had a room in a house connected with the clinic run by Dr Spitz. There were other women staying in this particular house whose children were also receiving treatment. The procedure you went through seems rather radical. Two "burr-holes" were drilled through your skull so that instruments could be inserted to examine the surface of your brain. The holes can still be felt today. We feel that this procedure plus the massive pain that you must have suffered have made you very sensitive to pressure of any description on your head. It has always been almost impossible to get you to wear a hat and for many years you hated getting your head wet. Showers were a problem, bringing an obvious statement of displeasure. The examination showed that there was still some dormant meningitis infection present. A cortisone derivative was prescribed to combat this. It was administered through spinal injection and would have been no party. As often happens with use of Cortizone you became slightly bloated in appearance. While you and Mary were away the people in the church helped a great deal with looking after Paul and Stephen.

Your capacity for responding to affection has been obvious over the years. As you grew up you responded to hugs and enjoyed giving them. This is still the case with the family. It's taken a long time to try to encourage you to be more discerning as to who you actually hug. People sometimes wonder at a complete stranger wanting to give them a big hug. Well again that seems enough for one letter so it is time to finish. I will write again because there is a lot more to tell.

Love Dad

$\mathcal{Letter}$ 9

Time at San Diego comes to an end.
The next step – moving to Denver.
Comments on the value of the Doman- Delacato Programme

Dear Mark,

It is been a while since I last wrote so here goes. During 1969 it became obvious that our time in San Diego was coming to an end. In an earlier letter I mentioned that when we moved to America I had notions of doing more study. While in San Diego I arranged with the University of California Extension Department and the University of Queensland to complete the last two subjects of my Bachelor of Arts with Queensland. While in San Diego I completed one subject and started on the final one which happened to be Introduction to Psychology. Mary did a Bookkeeping Course at nights with Adult Education and with her aptitude in Maths did extremely well. Pacific Beach United Methodist Church started to have trouble meeting its budget and began to consider cost-cutting. When I was appointed as Associate Pastor, the church was at a point in development where there was really too much for one minister to do successfully, and they decided to split the work as indicated in my job description. I guess they hoped the congregation would grow when there was a minister of evangelism which did happen to some extent but not enough to meet the costs involved. It was an awkward time and it became clear to us that it was time to move on, but where to and what about your program. Mary felt that there was more progress that could be made if you continued with the various activities and felt very reluctant to remove you from it. My own thoughts were that you had received the maximum benefit possible. We came to San Diego with high hopes that you would be restored to at least some of your original individual potential and you had made progress in some areas, the toilet training and general socialisation being good examples of progress, but the extent of your brain damage worked against the effectiveness of the program. We have never regretted that we made the effort to have you involved. The exposure you had to other people through the patterning was valuable in itself.

There is an excellent seminary in California at Claremont and I made enquiries there. I would have needed scholarship help and some sort of student pastorate and neither was available. The District Superintendent of the United Methodist Church was very helpful and suggested The Iliff School of Theology in Denver, Colorado, as a possibility. I made contact there and discovered that they would offer scholarship help, but the only student pastorates were a long way from the Seminary, and if we were to get any help with your care and training we needed to be close to Denver itself. The final decision to move was forced on us when the Pacific Beach Church indicated that they could no longer support us. It was a difficult moment and I think Mary thought that we were letting you down and I had more than a slight sense of failure as a minister of evangelism. The next step was to prepare to leave. There was packing to be done and a U-Haul van to be hired. We had greatly enjoyed our time at Pacific Beach and at the church in particular. We had made some great friends and remain in touch with one family. I hate farewells and find them very sad but the one which was arranged greatly helped the process. Marte Chamness, who I've mentioned before, very creatively organised the event. It started with a strawberry and ice cream evening. The fresh strawberries had been brought in. Americans love making ice cream in a churn which is what happened on that occasion. Instead of farewell speeches different groups of people had prepared skits depicting various incidents, mostly humorous, which had occurred during the three years. At the end we were presented with a leather folder which Marte had put together which included a whole range of memorabilia, church bulletins and notices of functions at Wesley Palms and a number of slides taken at various functions we had attended. We also received a bag with a generous amount of money. At some stage before we left we asked my father to look for an original bark painting to present to the church as a way of expressing appreciation to the congregation with something distinctively Australian. As far as I know it is an authentic and well executed piece so is appreciating in monitory value. The real point is that we had and have a genuine affection for the church and for San Diego itself.

This will seem like an old-time travelogue but as we head out of San Diego to the east in our monstrous Ford V8 pulling our U-Haul trailer it is a good time to finish this letter. We were opening a new chapter in your life and the life of our family.

Love Dad

Letter 10

Trip from San Diego to Denver. Mary and Noel finding jobs in Denver. A hair raising incident when Mark becomes lost after getting out of the car. Settling into accommodation at Iliff. Finding activities for Paul and Stephen and our first experience of snow.

In the last letter we were heading East from San Diego to Denver. At the time you were five years old, Stephen seven and Paul nine. The memories of the trip have become rather vague except that we spent the last night at a campground at Castle Rock just an hour or so from Denver. I guess it stands out in my memory as some five years later Paul, Stephen and I rode bikes there and spent a rather uncomfortable night in the campground. It was a far more difficult ride them we anticipated as there is a rather steep climb up to the town. All that we really knew was that we had accommodation in a unit on the campus of Iliff School of Theology in Denver, that they would provide some scholarship help towards fees while I studied and that Denver was on the eastern slopes of the Rockies. Indeed we found out when we got there that it is known as "the mile high city" and there are a number of points around the city where there are signs indicating that at that particular location it is exactly 1 mile high. Where there is a clear vantage point to the west it is possible to see the Rockies which are snow capped. It is a beautiful city with lots of trees. We had the address of the government run employment service and I seem to recall that we went there first as both Mary and I needed to find jobs. We went in, in turn. Mary found a job with Morse Chain Company as Time

Keeper, her bookkeeping course immediately paying off. I had to have an evening job so that I could look after you in the daytime. There was a job going as a cleaner with Blue Cross and Blue Shield from 5.30 in the afternoon till 9.30 at night. I had absolutely no cleaning experience and had been a rather fastidious youth with little desire to get my hands dirty, particularly when it came to cleaning things such as toilets. I got the job and when I began working it was a rapid learning experience. My workmates had great fun as I learnt to use a dust mop, a wet mop and bucket, and a buffer or floor polisher. When I was in the employment agency Mary started to tidy up the wagon. You quietly climbed out a window and when she turned round you were nowhere to be seen. We were in an absolute panic as you had neither sense of direction or danger. We looked around the parking lot and the nearby streets – no Mark. We then went back into the building and told someone what had happened. They gave us the number of the nearest police station. When we called them they informed us that someone had taken you to a nearby hospital. They had seen you wandering across Broadway, one of the main roads in Denver, realised of course that this should not be happening and had taken you to the hospital and phoned the police. To say that we were relieved would be the understatement of all time. It is one of a series of remarkable escape stories which involve yourself. As I mentioned in an earlier letter, if the door or gate was open you went through it, as hyperactivity was part of the aftermath of brain damage from meningitis. When we reached the Iliff School of Theology I went and made myself known and was told where the block of units was and given the name of the lady who managed them. Eventually we got to our unit on the second floor. The husband of the family beneath who was working on a Doctoral program was very helpful as we unloaded all our stuff and lugged it upstairs. His wife was also studying. I'm afraid as time went on they were not so helpful and complained to the business manager about the noise we made early in the morning. You always woke early and started to move around and we found it difficult to suppress the noise. It was not a good idea to put us on the second floor but that was the unit which was available. Those problems led, after some time, to our being located in a two story house the school owned, and which was far better suited to our needs, but more about that later. The unit had a living room, a kitchen area, bathroom and bedroom area. We divided the bedroom area with large cupboards so that you were on one side Paul and Stephen on the other. Mary and I had a divan bed in the living room. The unit was comfortable but not really ideal for a family the size of ours. As with every place we've lived in we had to try to "Mark proof" it. As I have pointed out, through no fault of your own, you needed to move constantly and love getting into things. You have always enjoyed getting things onto the floor and moving them around with your hands, cutlery, cereal, sugar, flour, you name it. We had to put hooks on drawers and cupboards which were not lockable. There was a garbage disposal unit under the sink as was the case in every home in America. The idea is to put soft garbage, food scraps etc. into the sink, run the tap and turn on the unit. The scraps get ground up and become liquid waste. There is some sort of rubber thing with divided edges to discourage hard objects from dropping down. It is possible for anyone to mistakenly leave hard objects in the sink so that they move into the garbage disposal and this was one of your fortes. I think we still have at least one teaspoon which bears the marks of the garbage disposal. I remember this happening in the unit in Denver but Mary informs me it started in San Diego. If one forgot to check for hard objects before turning it on there would be a horrible grinding sound and sometimes the whole thing would jam up. I didn't mean to get lost in the strengths and weaknesses of a garbage disposal unit but the grinding sound seemed to be a particular feature of the time in the unit.

We arrived in Denver during the long summer vacation so that we had some time to look for a school for Paul and Stephen, but also heard of a good program at Schlessman Y.M.C.A. which offered a number of activities for them. Two I remember are swimming and T-ball, a version of softball. For some reason I remember going to a swimming competition involving children of the program and Stephen being in a butterfly event. He hadn't quite learned to do the stroke but showing the determination of which he is very capable, he did the length of the pool using mainly his arms with his legs dragging under him as he was almost vertical. Both Paul and Stephen showed good aptitude for swimming and most other sports. We feel sure that you would have been just as capable. In your younger days you had well-developed calf muscles. Your brothers used to say that they were the best in the family and indicate that you would have been a runner. Of course, you do run quite fast and without seeming to get tired, thanks to your hyperactivity, but sadly have problems with coordination and direction. You have varied in your response to swimming over the years but mostly have enjoyed it.

Mary and I decided at some stage after you had meningitis and were so seriously affected that even though you would demand a lot of extra attention we would make every effort to ensure that this did not limit the range of activities in which Paul and Stephen would be involved. I think we succeeded and were glad to do so but it was not without the expending of a good deal of time and energy, particularly on Mary's part. We found that there was a special school which you could attend, although this was not at the beginning of our stay in Denver. It was a great plus that they had a bus which picked you up and brought you home.

It was while we were staying in the unit that we had our first experience of snow. I have a set of slides which I took from the veranda of the block of units at various times of the day as more and more snow came down. We loved the way snow transforms the landscape, with its clinging to trees and buildings and the way it softens noise. The sound of traffic is reduced after a fall of snow. We didn't enjoy driving in it. Even with studded snow tires, when the roads get icy, and although taking a great deal of care, it is still possible to slide off the road or into the gutter or even do a 360° turn – all hair raising stuff. It was also no fun clearing the paths and sidewalk near ones house. Mary will tell you that she did a lot of shovelling of snow when I wasn't around. Because of Denver's height, even though there are sometimes quite heavy falls, the snow doesn't stay around for long forming drifts, which was a great advantage.

You could say that this letter has been an introduction to our stay in Denver. When we went there it was with the thought that we would stay two or three years but we finished up staying for five. Five very full, almost crazy years, in terms of what we were all doing but more of this in the next letter.

Love Dad

Davis Family

Paul

Mary, Mark, Noel

Stephen

A recent photo (2018) of the family. Paul and Stephen live at Ouribah and Melbourne.

Mary and Mark with a dolphin at Seaworld for Mark's fortieth. The dolphin was also 40.

Letter 11

The family in Denver. Accidents involving Mark.
Establishing a safe area for Mark in the house.

Dear Mark,

I'll add a bit more in this letter about our time in Denver. Mary was working full-time at Morse Chain about half an hour's drive from where we were living. She had a responsible job as Time keeper and later as Pay clerk, which she performed very well with her expertise and conscientiousness. Once I completed my BA I was able to start on the Master of Divinity program and receive some credits for the work I had done in the Diploma of Divinity with Queensland University and the subjects at King's College. I was doing the equivalent of a full-time student and eventually was working as a cleaner for some 40 hours a week. We had to tell Paul and Stephen that if they wanted anything extra in the way of bikes etc. they would need to get part-time jobs. They both had paper routes. In other words, they delivered papers morning and night. This was good training in business for them as they had to keep a record of papers delivered, make out accounts and then go round and collect the money owed at the end of each month. It was also rather difficult to deliver the papers in bad weather, which meant not only folding or rolling the papers but also putting plastic around them. When it was snowing it was not possible to ride the special paper bikes so there was experimentation with pulling some sort of sled, but I think they just pushed the bike through the snow. Maybe it is this experience which started them in the direction, work wise, in which they have both gone, into business. Later in our stay they sometimes helped in the cleaning business but more of that in another letter. Neither Mary nor I can remember a lot of details about the school you attended every day but they would have worked on things such as coordination and manipulative skills. I'm very grateful to the family for allowing my involvement in more study, particularly Mary. In going back to full-time study I was doing what had come to be something urgent and vital.

The hours spent in cleaning gradually increased partially motivated by a desire not to have the family suffer a great deal of financial deprivation. The cleaning at Blue Cross and Blue Shield was eventually supplemented by occasional work with the cleaning business run by Joe O'Connell and then establishing our own cleaning business but more of that in another letter.

I have very vivid memories of one incident while we were living in the apartment. We had to be very careful where we placed things which could be dangerous as one does for any child. Since we had trouble training you, and you basically wanted to do the things carried out by a two-year-old we had to be particularly careful. You also move very fast. One day while Mary was at work I slipped up in this vigilance and left a cup of tea or coffee I had just poured too close to the edge of the kitchen bench. You reached up and pulled it over yourself. You were badly scalded. Naturally you tried to claw at your chest. I had some memory from somewhere of children doing more injury to themselves than through the actual burn by trying to get at the affected part and asked Paul and Stephen to restrain you while I went to the phone box to call the doctor. We then took you to the surgery. At that stage we didn't have a phone but had one installed soon after. This might be the time to talk about a few of the escapades in which you were involved. Paul and Stephen started to count the number of stitches you had in your head over the years which might sound a little morbid but you did have a number of visits to the doctor after falls. I think they got up to over 50. These sorts of accidents can happen to any child, but the possibilities were increased by your being uncoordinated due to your condition. You gradually became more stable as time went on and the tally of stitches, thankfully, pretty well ended. I mentioned earlier that we moved into a house owned by the school. This was a beautiful old house, two stories with an attic and a basement. The sad part about it was that it had been neglected to some extent in that the timber used on the staircase and around the doors and windows had been painted for ease of maintenance. It was set on a large and fenced block of land which joined up with another even larger house belonging to the school. Right across the road was a fairly large park. It was a tremendous relief to have the space which the house afforded after the apartment. The bottom floor was made up of a huge interconnected lounge and dining room, bathroom and large kitchen from which there was a staircase to the basement and another smaller room which served as a laundry. Upstairs there were four bedrooms. You had the one at the head of the stairs. Stephen was in the first bedroom at the front of the house, Mary and I in the next one and Paul in the one at the end of the hallway. The bathroom was between yours and Paul's bedroom and there was a door leading from there to a few steps which led to the attic. There was a big old building at the back which was very neglected and was probably the original coachhouse. Paul and Stephen eventually used it as their paper route office, and mostly folded papers there and loaded up their bikes. I've spent a bit of time describing the house as various parts of it are involved in your escapades. I've also mentioned the process of "Mark proofing" the various houses we lived in so that you could have an area in which to move freely, where everything you liked to play with was located and was closed off from other rooms where the rest of the family's things could be intact. Your particular area in the house in Denver consisted of a large entranceway, the staircase, your bedroom and the rather long hallway from which the other bedrooms and bathroom opened out. All these doors had special catches beyond your reach. As I write it all sounds rather grim and I don't want to give the impression of a prison. When the rest of the family were in various rooms to keep an eye on what you were doing you were very welcome and, of course, we always had meals together. This particular set up was necessary to preserve our sanity. It is hard to describe to the average person what it is like to live with someone who is affected with the type of hyperactivity which can be the result of brain damage. It was a matter of the rest of the family learning to adapt and finding ways of coping. At the same time we wanted you to develop to your potential which had certainly been greatly reduced by the meningitis. I was going to write about some of your escapades in this letter but it is taken me more space than I thought to give the setting so will finish up here and continue in the next.

Love Dad

Letter 12

Mark's escapades in our house in Denver.

Dear Mark,

In the last letter I spoke of the house we lived in for about four years in Denver, the setting for some of your escapades. It's hard to know where to start. It was difficult for the family to remember to always lock the bedroom doors or other doors leading off your special area. So there was a time when the door to the bedroom, which had a window opening onto the roof of the entranceway to the house, was left open. I was at the side of the house playing with Paul and Stephen when one of us noticed that you had crawled out of the window onto the roof and were moving towards the edge from which there was about a 10 foot drop onto a cemented area. I bolted round as fast as I could in the hopes of getting there to catch you. It's almost like a bad dream as I didn't make it. You crashed down. The details of what happened next have faded but you didn't sustain any broken bones and were not knocked out. You had no sense of fear so you were completely relaxed as you fell. We certainly would have taken you to the doctor to make sure you had no concussion and then kept a close eye on you to notice any unusual reactions. We always felt a certain sense of guilt when something like this happened as we had not been able to prevent the incident. I think it was after this that we asked the school if wire could be attached on the inside of the window frames so that this could not happen again and they agreed. It was sometime after this that there was a similar but much worse event. The outside of the house was being painted and as the painters reached each room the wire was removed from the windows. So it was that one day when the door to one of the bedrooms at the side of the house was left unlocked you crawled out the window. There was nothing between the upstairs window and the ground. The first indication of what had happened was when Mary, who was sitting in one of the downstairs rooms saw you hurtling past the window. You were unconscious when she got to you but with no obvious breaks. She called the Dr who met her at the hospital and you were admitted overnight for observation. We think you had fallen at least 15 feet but again had done so in such a relaxed fashion that there were no serious injuries. You left the hospital the next day as the staff felt that you were over the worst after-effects, but we think you slept for some 2 to 3 days, which was far from usual.

Then there was the incident which caused the greatest local drama. I was at a job I had on a Sunday when this happened. The attic was not used a great deal but Paul and Stephen would sometimes play there. On this particular Sunday the door to the bathroom had been left unhooked and the door to the attic couldn't be locked. At some stage during the day one of the neighbours came over and asked Mary if she knew Mark was up on the roof. Of course, she didn't. You had made your way out of the attic window and proceeded to walk across the roof. Mary and Paul raced up to see what they could do. It was raining and the roof which had wooden tiles had become quite slippery. Paul who was about 14 at the time and Mary crawled out to where you were but were not able to move with you because of the state of the roof. Mary left you with Paul and went down to call the fire brigade which is what one does in such circumstances in America. They came with sirens blaring. You can see why this incident caused considerable local drama. They put the ladder up and then went out on the roof. Mary and Paul were very impressed with the way they handled the situation. Rather than just lifting you up and carrying you back to the attic, one moved a few steps away and then passed you from one to the other and so on until you were safe, a tremendous relief. I took great pleasure in nailing the attic door closed.

There is just one other great escapade I'll mention. This must have happened in the year before we returned to Australia. Mary recalls that her mother, your Grandma Buckle and your stepgrandfather, Cec. were staying with us. You managed to get out of one of the downstairs windows and suddenly someone noticed that you were missing. This was another time I was not present. The family fanned out in all directions. Stephen and a friend who were riding bikes eventually found you in a park about a mile away. Fortunately you had gone left rather than right when you moved away from the house, otherwise you would have made your way across a four-lane highway.

Every family has hair raising incidents as children learn their way through life and the whole family meets varying circumstances, but I guess what I have described as your escapades are made more telling by your ongoing dependence and inability to learn from them. I was thinking about similar incidents involving the other boys in the younger days and remembered that Paul as a toddler had a wanderlust. Fortunately, we had a dog called Minnie at the time, a black shaggy dog of no particular breed, who had wandered into our place at Oakey and we had given it a home. The dog and Paul were inseparable so where Paul was so was the dog. If Paul went missing Mary would go out and call Minnie and where she came from would indicate Paul's whereabouts. At one stage that was the kitchen of a neighbour's house.

That's probably enough for one letter. You did keep us on our toes, so to speak, as you gradually grew up and showed an amazing ability to survive. We had to learn to adapt to your condition but have sometimes wondered what you would have been like. As you grew up you were very open in showing affection. You love giving people a big hug. It is great with the family to have you charging up to greet us calling our names and then giving us a massive bear hug. It's interesting that in spite of the apparent limitations on your memory you have not forgotten your brothers even though now that we all live in different locations you only see them occasionally. Your response is to call them by the names you use, Pore and Stea, and to give them a big hug. You were thrown on one occasion when you saw Paul for the first time with a beard, however as soon as he spoke you recognised him. I seem to be rambling again so will sign off.

Love Dad

Letter 13

Mark's taking of drugs. A bit more about epilepsy. The reactions of many other people to those with handicaps. Mark's apparent unawareness of his handicap and his ingestion of chewing gum. Mark's teeth and visits to the dentist. Appreciation of music.

Moving on from the hair raising experiences I spoke about in the last letter. Over the years, from the time you had meningitis and as an aftermath suffering from epilepsy and hyperactivity, you had to take a number of different drugs in an effort to control these effects. We learned early that no one can really predict exactly what the individual's reaction will be to any particular drug or what the exact dosage should be. There is, of course, the general understanding of what each drug should do and of possible side-effects. What doctors were looking for was a balance of drugs which would help control the hyperactivity and epilepsy without slowing your actions too much. It was really a matter of trial and error. The doctors would prescribe particular drugs and the dosage then we would report to them what was happening. When you were on Dilantin we found that eventually your gums began to thicken up so that the whole of your teeth were not exposed. The dosage was gradually reduced. There were a couple of occasions when through the build up of drugs in your system, your level of coordination dropped, and you mostly wanted to sleep. This sort of build up would happen at times when you were constipated. Running a temperature would also increase the likelihood of seizure activity. It would be impossible to calculate the number of tablets and capsules you have taken over the years so that we are very fortunate that you take them so easily. At first it was suggested to Mary that she put the tablets in your mouth and hold your nose and force you to swallow them. The addition of butter and jam was also tried but then you got to the stage where you just swallowed them after they were put in your mouth. Today, when tablets are set out in front of you, as you pick them up one or two at a time, you say, "one, two" and so on. Some of the tablets seem to have caused you dryness of mouth so that you become constantly thirsty. This seems to have become less of a problem as you have grown older.

This is probably a good time to talk about the reactions of people to somebody like yourself. It is a natural reaction to give extra attention to someone or something which is different. I guess it's mainly curiosity, but it's not always helpful if people stare at someone who is handicapped in any way. There have been many times over the years when we have been out with you that we were conscious of people staring so that we developed a response of just ignoring the attention and going on with whatever we happened to be doing. Children are perhaps the most likely to stare which is understandable. You see, you walk in a rather uncoordinated fashion, and we have always needed to either take you by the arm, or as you've got older, encourage you to take our arm in case you get the urge to run off. Now that you're older the urge to run away is non-existent. In your younger days you would extend your arm as you moved through a shopping centre and maybe knock things off shelves or touch people, and people in general are very sensitive about random touching. You developed a liking for chewing gum and lollies and would grab these from shelves and carry on when they had to be put back, as any child would. The difference is that, in effect, no matter what your actual age might be, you always behave as a two-year-old because of the brain damage, so that waiting has been a problem. Some of the stares we have received have about them a tinge of," why don't those people do something about that person's behaviour". As a family we all had to come to terms with the excessive attention, but it was more difficult for Paul and Stephen. They have, over the years, been very accepting of you introducing you to friends they brought home and explaining the situation. Indeed this has been a very positive effect of your intellectual handicap, in that it has made us all aware of what it means to have someone with a handicap of any description in a family and therefore raise the level of our compassion. It has enabled us to be more accepting of people with disabilities. There is a certain wariness or even fear towards people with disabilities, particularly those of an intellectual nature, if one is unfamiliar with them. With us as a family, this has long since gone, thanks to having you in the family. We know that Paul and Stephen have matured into particularly compassionate and sensitive people through their close association with you over the years.

This is probably the time to mention that we have considered it some sort of perverse blessing that you seem unaware of the difference which exists between yourself and most other people. In other words, you are not aware of your disability, and certainly not aware of the possible adverse attitudes of others. Over the years we have known a number of more mildly intellectually handicapped people who are aware of their lack of ability, and very aware of the attitudes of those around them. We have felt for them, feeling their sense of loss and their desire to be different. It is always great when such people with the care, understanding and guidance of others come to accept themselves as they are and work to explore their potential. This, of course is no different for any individual, but the difficulties are greater for those with disabilities.

I mentioned earlier that you developed a liking for chewing gum and many sorts of lollies. When we travel, Mary and I like to have various munchies on hand, particularly nuts and gum, and Paul and Stephen therefore shared in consuming some of these. This meant, of course, that when things were going round you had your share. The problem is that you have never learnt to just chew gum and eventually dispose of it. You chew it and swallow it. Since we have done a great deal of travelling wherever we've been, you have swallowed a veritable mountain of gum during your lifetime, but it doesn't seem to have affected your health. We have, of course, always cleaned your teeth, an activity you learnt to enjoy but you have never learnt to rinse your mouth out, so that the only thing to do was to give you a drink after teeth cleaning so that the toothpaste is washed down. Again, it doesn't seem to have affected your health. Talking about teeth – the Davis teeth are wide spaced, thanks, I guess, to my mother who had such a gap in her teeth that she had a plate made with an extra tooth on it. The gene for spacing is very dominant in our case, as my sister Joan and I both had fairly large spaces between our teeth and we both had a thing about it, wanting to grin rather than have a smile showing teeth. The same spacing has been passed on to you three boys and to Joan's children, Glenys and Jennifer. Paul and Stephen are fortunate in having a good combination of their mothers and my teeth so that there is some spacing but their teeth are straight. I have to say that you were not so fortunate in that you have large spaces and your teeth are crooked. However both you and I rejoice that, thanks to the spacing, we don't have a lot of trouble with decay. This has not saved you from an occasional trip to the dentist. This has never been easy. It has not been possible to explain to you that what is going to happen is for the best, and as far as you are concerned someone unfamiliar is causing you to sit in one place for some time, forcing your mouth open, and also causing at the very least some discomfort and pain. This is a background to saying it has never been a party taking you to the dentist. I can recall Mary and I having to keep your legs and arms still and the dentist putting some sort of special rubber object at the edge of your jaws so that you're not able to clamp your teeth shut. Eventually it was discovered that the best way to handle dental problems is to give you an anaesthetic and then carry out whatever work has to be done. Having your hair cut was not a lot easier. You have always hated any pressure on your head. We think that Mary cut your hair in San Diego, as she cut all our hair in Fiji. We can't seem to remember what happened in Denver but do have a good memory of going to the barber when we came back to Frankston in Melbourne. The barber whom I went to myself agreed to cut your hair. We would take you in right after he had closed for the day. We would stand each side of you and one would hold your arms down and the other keep your head still. Again the major problem was that we were not able to explain that all of this was for your benefit. We would keep stuffing jellybeans into your mouth which activity had two purposes, first of all, it kept you happy and it also prevented you from bellowing. Jeff, the barber, would then proceed to cut your hair as quickly as possible. Now that you're in a house with three or four other severely intellectually handicapped people we think that your carers have somebody come in to cut your hair.

You have always responded to music even though television has never been a real interest. Probably because of the shortness of your attention span, thanks to the brain damage, sitting and watching TV programs has not been your favourite activity. The most likely aspect of TV to interest you has been the ads., We think because of the increased colour and sound, and perhaps the brevity. We noticed that when we were watching TV if you are sitting down with us you would pay more attention to our reactions to what was going on. As I mentioned earlier you learnt nursery rhymes during the patterning in San Diego and always enjoyed a particular nursery rhyme LP which we played ad-infinitum, it seems. You mostly wandered around while it was on but were obviously paying attention as, no sooner had it finished, that you indicated you wanted it played again and never tired of it. We enjoy music as a family. Mary and I listen to classical music most of the day. Paul and Stephen also enjoy classical music but have interest in a range of modern music. Both showed considerable aptitude in playing musical instruments. Paul became very proficient for a time on the violin, Stephen the cello. This is probably an aptitude which you would also have possessed.

This letter has really blown out, so to speak, so will finish here with lots more to come.

Love Dad

Letter 14

*More about life in Denver. Mark's enjoyment of being
in a car. Camping trips while in Denver.*

A bit more about life in Denver where we finished up spending
five years. We tried to get away for holidays, wherever possible,
to places where we could camp within Colorado, and there are
some which stand out in my memory. You have always enjoyed
being in a car. I'm not sure what it is that appeals to you and
have often wondered about it. Possibly it's the motion of the car
or vehicle or maybe the closeness of other people; but I don't
think it's the latter as you tend to ignore those around you in a
social situation. You do like to be on the move so that when we
have driven somewhere and have got out to look at something
or just to eat, as soon as the food is gone you will say "car"
indicating that you want to get going. When we were getting
ready to leave Melbourne in Australia, we needed to check out
a house in Brisbane and had limited time so that we drove the
1500 km with just necessary stops. After a few hours sleep we
looked at the house and then set out to drive back. On that day
we drove about 800 km and stopped in a motel. We had no
sooner got inside than you said "car" and wanted to get going
again. We have noticed that most intellectually handicapped
people also enjoy being in a vehicle. Over the years we tried
to point out various things for you to see, such as animals we
were passing, without capturing your interest. However there
was a stage when you would say, "swing", when we passed a
playground as this was something you enjoyed, and "plane"

when you saw one. Quite often, nobody else in the car had seen the plane, so that you were very observant.

There was one particular camping trip which became a tradition for us. On Thanksgiving Day weekend we would get our camping gear together and head out to Cherry Creek Reservoir campground on the outskirts of Denver. Since it was well into winter we had the whole campground to ourselves and a couple of times camped in the snow. The reservoir would be partly frozen over. We had a couple of Coleman catalytic heaters which were quite effective so that the tent was quite cosy at nights. We've had a dog wherever we've been. Towards the end of our stay in Denver we had a German Shepherd – Husky cross we called Duke. We had picked him up from the pound. He was a beautiful dog but not very sensible, and if ever he had the chance would take off, and since he loved to chase cars would do so even if it meant being in the middle of the traffic on a busy road. On one of our camps at Cherry Creek Paul and Stephen decided to use him to pull firewood to the campsite, so they harnessed him up to some quite large pieces of wood which he managed to pull along with relative ease. This was the Husky coming out in him. He had spasms when his back legs wouldn't be able to move, and eventually we discovered that he had a form of epilepsy, so that you and he had something in common. When we left Denver we had to find a home for him, and were fortunate to find someone who had a large property and who as a nurse understood the epilepsy problem. The whole family have fond memories of our stays at Cherry Creek Reservoir.

There was another of our weekend camping trips which could be called the camping trip from Hell. It was also to a lake so we took along our fishing gear. My memory of the actual location is rather hazy but I can recall that the campground was rather crowded. You got a marshmallow caught in your throat which we tried to dislodge by putting our arms around your stomach area and giving quick squeezes and by even holding you upside down neither of which worked. Mary managed to get it out by putting a finger down your throat, not a pleasant experience.

We decided to try our hand at fishing. The lake was surrounded by rocks so we made our way across and threw in our lines. At one stage Mary was sitting behind Stephen, I think, holding you and Stephen in the act of casting brought the line behind him and the hook got caught in the top of Mary's head. The line broke so Mary was left with a hook in her scalp with a short length of line hanging from it. We couldn't see how we could get the hook out, so started to head up the rocks, aiming to go to the emergency section of the local hospital about 25 miles away. The rocks were slippery and you slipped over and cut your head. We held a cloth to the cut to stop the bleeding and proceeded to the hospital. When we got there it was to discover that there had been a major car accident in which a number of people was seriously injured, so that they suggested we get something to eat and come back later. We traipsed into a shop somewhere, Mary with a hook in her head and you with a cut on your forehead. When we eventually got into the emergency room, you got some stitches in your head and the doctor removed the hook by pushing it through, cutting off the barbed end and then pulling it out. Mary has always said that it wasn't particularly painful as it was in her scalp, but she is made of much sterner stuff than me.

On another holiday we headed for Steamboat Lake. Joe O'Connell had bought a Canadian type canoe which he loaned to us. I'm always reluctant to borrow things from people as it has been my experience that if anything is to go wrong with the particular article it will be while I'm using it. Joe persuaded me and as he never did anything by halves also loaned me a book on the use of a canoe so we could read up about how to paddle and the various strokes designed to keep the canoe going straight or to turn it. We had no trouble transporting it, as we still had our Ford V8 station wagon with a large hood rack. We found Steamboat Lake to be a beautiful place. I seem to remember huge grassy areas around the lake with the possibility of pitching the tent anywhere. We took the canoe out a great deal and became quite proficient in its use, even doing some fishing from it. I have a classic slide somewhere of Paul running towards me through a field of yellow flowers. All that was the good part of the trip. Sometimes events are etched in one's mind by mishaps and that was the case with this trip. We were on the way back home feeling relaxed and happy when I had to stop the car to adjust the front rope holding the canoe in place. We had bought a little dog with us from San Diego. A lady in the church had given him to us. He was black with fairly long hair, possibly having a bit of terrier in him. With a great deal of creativity we had called him Aussi. He was very much a part of family. When I stopped the car he managed to jump out of an open window and tried to run across a very busy highway. He was hit by a car which must have been going at some 70 miles an hour and killed instantly. I can still see it. For some reason I decided to bury him beside the road and had great trouble digging a shallow grave as the ground was so hard. We were very sad to lose him and Paul and Stephen sobbed the rest of the way home.

The last holiday or perhaps I should say trip we had from Denver was when we had decided it was time to move back to Australia and more about that in another letter. Your grandmother and step grandfather, Mary's mother and Cec. had come to stay with us as part of the last stage of a world trip. We decided that we wanted to see something of the eastern half of America having had the big trip around the National Parks from San Diego. I had to arrange to have the various cleaning jobs covered and we had limited time. We were away for about three weeks and in that time went as far south as Florida and then north as far as Washington, New York, the Niagara Falls and then west through Chicago so that we could at least touch the Great Lakes, and through the corn belt of the Mid West. This was a saga in itself so I will only write about some of the highlights. We had bought a second hand Star Craft trailer, the sort which opens, winds up and has pull out ends. It slept eight. At that stage we had a Volvo station wagon. I had been forced to trade in the V8 wagon. As we set out on a trip we had seven people and were pulling a trailer. It was a lot to ask of the Volvo but it did very well. Mostly Paul and Stephen travelled in the back of the wagon which was made more comfortable with sleeping bags. We would never be permitted to travel with such an arrangement today. Paul and Stephen were 15 and 13 and you were 11. As adolescents your brothers were not over happy about travelling with a bunch of older people. However as they look back on it they're glad to have gone to some of the places we visited. There were a couple of mishaps. You put your finger in a fan in a shop in New Orleans much to the consternation of the shop owner, mainly because he thought he would be sued. Fortunately it didn't need stitching. Stephen managed to get the end of the brake lever of a dual bike into the muscle of his leg as he and Paul were having a great time. This did need some stitches. Highlights, other than the country we saw was swimming at Fort Pearce in Florida, beautifully warm and, of course in the Atlantic, the Empire State building, Statue of Liberty and UN building in New York, the Niagara

Falls – absolutely awe-inspiring, and finally being on the edge of a tornado, fortunately just the edge, in Nebraska. The USA is a vast country and one becomes very aware of its size on a trip like this. One has the same concept of size while driving in Australia. We didn't see everything we wanted to but have always been glad we made the effort.

Well, son that's it for the holidays and trips so for now I will sign off.

Love Dad

Letter 15

Sunday School for Mark. Our own cleaning business.
When toilet training misfired. Mark's activities.

Dear Mark,

As I spoke about the big trip we had through Central and Eastern America I mentioned that we were thinking about returning to Australia. That episode in itself with what led up to it will probably take a couple of letters and there are a few other things to cover about the stay in Denver.

Pretty well every Sunday from 9.30 to 11.15 am Mary took you to a special education class at University Park United Methodist Church. It was located right across from Denver University and Iliff School of theology. Mary was able to attend church, Paul and Stephen Sunday school, although Paul sometimes played the violin at the special education class and we have an article from the Rocky Mountain United Methodist paper to prove it. Indeed you also feature in another article. The class was run at the time by a very remarkable lady, Marilyn Stoddart. It originated in 1955 and was run under the auspices of the Denver Council of Churches. The students were physically or mentally handicapped, or both, with an age range of 10 to 35 with varying ability. Marilyn managed to gain the involvement of a number of people as carers as the group needed almost 1 to 1. They used quite a lot of music, hence Paul's involvement. Wherever possible participants were encouraged to read Bible passages, sing hymns and take part in other acts of worship. The aims were to develop an idea of God and to talk to him, to encourage the participants to express themselves through music, art and dance and above all to feel a sense of personal worth and dignity.

For the last couple of years we established a cleaning business. Joe O'Connell who I've mentioned a couple of times suggested that if one wanted to make money from cleaning, it was the way to go. I did suggest earlier that one of my aims was to try to prevent the family suffering too much financially, bolstered, I have to say, by a fair degree of ambition. The business was called 5D Janitorial Service – 5D because there are five Davises and it was cleaning to the fifth dimension. When we started Mary gave up her job at Morse chain to work with me. At the time I had given up my part-time job with Blue Cross and Blue Shield and was cleaning a couple of floors at the Petroleum Club Building in downtown Denver. The lady in charge agreed to let Mary and I clean five floors. The main reason I've spoken of this is to indicate the support I had from the total family and how much responsibility we expected and got from your brothers. For most of the time we had the Petroleum Club, Mary, Stephen and I would leave home about 5:30 PM and start cleaning. Paul would therefore be looking after you. About 8 PM I would go with Stephen to a bus not far from the building and he would travel back home. Mary and I would continue to work sometimes till 1 AM. There was one night when we got home that we thought the whole system had collapsed. Stephen wasn't there and Paul told us what had happened. Near the front door as one came into the entrance was a wooden grate, a ventilator for the heating system. On this particular night the grate was out as you had recently had a painting episode, more about that a little later. Stephen managed to slip into that opening and taught the top of his leg on a protruding nail. It was obvious that he needed medical attention so Paul called a friend's place and one of the parents came round and took Stephen to emergency. We went up to the hospital to bring Stephen home. Eventually as I got contracts for other buildings we gave up to Petroleum Club. Paul and Stephen occasionally worked with me to earn pocket money. At one stage we were employing about four university students in various buildings. I was on a rapid learning curve as far as running a small business is concerned, and it gave me an appreciation of the stresses and strains involved. Mary worked at the headquarters of the Rocky Mountain conference of the United Methodist Church in the account section and enjoyed the company of her workmates greatly. We are aware of the enormous responsibility we were placing on Paul and Stephen, particularly Paul as the oldest and there were tensions but they have come out the other end of it is responsible, sensitive human beings. As the years have gone by we learnt that they had their way of making it easier for themselves. I mentioned earlier that they learnt to play musical instruments, Paul, the violin, Stephen, the cello and both became very proficient. They were supposed to practice regularly whether we were there or not. As we had no other way of checking, the system was that they were to switch on a tape recorder so that we would know if they had been practicing. They informed us, years down the track, that they spent the necessary time recording practice sessions for the two of them but banked on us not distinguishing that it was the same pieces being played all the time – and they were right.

I mentioned painting episodes. You were toilet trained, a huge step in your development but couldn't get to the toilet in your area so whoever was caring for you needed to check how you're going or hear you say "toi". There were a few times when you had a bowel movement which dropped out of your pants and you proceeded to finger paint with it very thoroughly. The bannister of the staircase was one place which could be painted, the grill of the ventilation system and the window at one of the landings which had 24 small panes. Cleaning up after an episode was a major undertaking, with buckets of water and loads of disinfectant, rags and a scrubbing brush. It was certainly something for which you could not be reprimanded as it could have been avoided.

On the whole you have a happy approach to life, loving to move, to run, to feel things that move, and run your fingers through them such as pieces of wool, string and pegs. You enjoyed having a yard to play in and used to collapse onto your knees and pull grass. There were attempts to train you out of this but without success. You no longer do this as you've got older. You enjoy listening to music in an unfocused way, and we found that you like having music boxes around, the ones which have a string to pull. Some carers you've you been associated with have felt that this should be discouraged as not being age-appropriate, but for years we had a couple in the car. As you grew up you loved to be chased around the place and to roughhouse particularly with Paul and Stephen. They would pick you up and toss you on a bed, when you would laugh and really enjoy it all. I get the impression that you associate these times with them when they see you. I mentioned your reaction to people other than family at one stage, and this is probably a good time to say something more about it. You generally ignore other people unless they are directly involved in some aspect of your care, such as helping you to eat or bath. There was never any desire to play with other children. Now that you're older you don't seem to pay a lot of attention to people around you other than those you know well. We've often been glad that you didn't grow to the same size as Paul and Stephen and are therefore easier to handle. You are about 5'8" but Paul is 6 foot four and Stephen 6 foot eight. We're not sure if the brain damage you suffered with meningitis affected the growth centre or this is the size you would have been. As you grew up we always had a large mirror in your bedroom as you enjoyed looking at it, and we're convinced that you considered this to be another person, not recognising this as yourself.

You developed a couple of characteristics which are not pleasant although understandable and there have been lots of attempts from a range of people to dissuade you from them without success. When you are prevented from doing something you want to do, or there isn't an immediate reaction to something you want, you growl quite loudly. There is no other way to describe the sound. It is a very definite way of expressing your feelings, given that you can't state in words what you want. The other unpleasant characteristic and this one has largely dropped away as I write this, is to grab someone with you by the front of their clothes in the chest region when you are not happy about something. This has usually been with women, particularly of course, Mary. We have all tried to stop you doing this and Paul, Stephen and myself have grabbed you by the wrist and squeezed to break your hold saying emphatically, "no, Mark". We're not sure where you picked up this action as it's not something that any of us do to one another. There is a level of frustration which builds up when caring for someone like yourself. It's terrible to have to say this, Mark, but I would be less than honest if I didn't mention it. There are frustrations in bringing up any child, the level depending on the personality and demeanour of the individual. This is compounded when someone is not able to understand what is desired, and has characteristics, such as extreme hyperactivity. In situations such as I've described above, breaking your hold on someone, we have at times reacted more strongly than was perhaps necessary. I've known situations with others where the frustration has led to actual physical harm to the handicapped person. This is, of course, tragic and not to be condoned but we do understand how it comes about. There are families which break up when faced with the differences which having a handicapped person bring. This didn't happen with us but there were strains on the family over the years and I'm extremely grateful that we stayed together.

This is another letter which is getting out of hand but it seems the right time to speak about sleeping patterns. Since you are hyperactive, without drugs, you probably would have run until you expired. As you got older you have settled down an enormous amount. One reason is that now you are 52 you have developed some arthritis which of course has slowed you down. We adopted the practice of getting you up in the middle of the night to take you to the toilet and try to avoid a wet bed and at that time, usually about 10 PM would give you more tablets. It was a great asset that you just swallowed them. Quite often you would have a seizure during the night and it was a matter of getting there as soon as possible so you wouldn't thud out of bed. It was an asset that I go to sleep very easily, so over the years it worked out better for me to get up in these situations, although when I was away Mary had to do it. A long time before the concentration on "cot death" I always checked that you and the other boys were breathing whenever I would come in after you were in bed, or when I had to get up in the night.

As usual in these letters one thing has led to another and we've covered a lot in this one so it's time to sign off.

Love Dad

Letter 16

Preparing to leave Denver and return to Australia.
Packing up. Travelling to the West coast.
The journey by ship across the Pacific.

Dear Mark,

In a previous letter I mentioned that we had realised it was time to leave Denver and that is really the major topic of this letter. It was in 1974. I said earlier that it was a crazy time in a way, considering all that we crammed into it. For me it was a great time as I followed out my study and explored the questions I had formed in my mind over the years but it did put enormous pressure on the family particularly on Mary. I think for us all the experiences we had, starting with Fiji were very broadening and led to a greater acceptance of people of different cultures. However, it became obvious it was time to move on, but where to? I had completed a Master of Divinity and all the preliminaries for a doctorate in theology and started on a thesis and worked like crazy to complete it, but knew it would need more time. I didn't have enough background to look for anything in the academic field and wasn't really sure that that was what I wanted. I knew I didn't want to go back into a parish at that stage. We thought about the possibility of going back to southern California which we loved but knew that your status with the Immigration Department would not allow us to visit Australia as a family or any other country and get back in. We felt it was time to get back closer to our families, having been away for 11 years. Your grandfather, Vic Davis, at my request started sending over cuttings from the employment sections of the local paper and church paper. I read about openings for school chaplains with the Council for Christian education in schools in Melbourne and applied. They indicated an interest but I'd need to be interviewed on our return. I then needed to sell the business, the equipment and goodwill, which finally came about, and the Volvo, which was no problem at all. We decided that it was to our advantage to go back by ship as we were entitled to a great deal of space in the hold. We had accumulated a considerable amount of stuff and decided we wanted to take the Star Craft back. A passage was booked on the Oriana to leave from San Francisco. It then became obvious that we could have trouble returning as a total family. Paul who was then 15 was not convinced he wanted to go back to Australia. The three of you had really grown up outside Australia and not one of you had any memory of it. We learned later that Paul had arranged to stay with friends and to support himself by washing dishes, I think, at the Denver University Canteen. There were a few incentives to going back which swung the decision towards the family. Paul and Stephen would share a cabin in the Oriana and therefore have a good measure of independence, and to get across the country with our stuff we would need to hire a U-Haul van and pull the Star Craft which was quite an adventure. The packing up was a major undertaking. In most places it's possible to buy tea chests or wooden boxes of some type for packing but these were not available in Denver. This meant that I had to make the boxes. Since I'm not particularly adept in the carpentry field or anything involving manual dexterity I made a couple of simple mistakes. I made one box down in the basement but since I hadn't measured the doorway in relation to the size of the box when it came time to take it out it wouldn't fit through the door so I had to start on that one again. We had an aluminium step ladder we wanted to take back and therefore needed quite a long box to accommodate it. When I measured the ladder I forgot to allow for the fact that one section of it was longer than the other when it was folded up. This meant that it wouldn't fit in the specially made box. In what is billed as the craziest thing I have ever done I grabbed a hacksaw and cut off the extra long bit of the ladder, roaring with laughter as I did it. That's how Mary found us when she came in from something she'd gone out to do. We used the ladder for some years. At the last minute we found out that it was not possible to ship anything in the Star Craft which meant a flurry of purchasing sheets of ply to contain the three bikes we had acquired. Fortunately each box had to have a metal band around it for which we had to hire a special device. I say fortunately, as when we got back to Australia the bands were about the only things holding some of the boxes together.

We had decided that we wanted to go back to Pacific Beach on the way home. This meant that we would drive to Los Angeles and unload there, where everything would be put on the Oriana. You and Mary would fly across a little later. We had a type of patio sale to try to sell some of the stuff we couldn't take back and also had to find homes for two cats and Duke as I mentioned earlier. The homes the animals went to seemed very caring. As the time to leave with the van and the trailer approached we discovered that because of the snow falls in the Rockies there was really only one pass we could negotiate. It was night when we left and I can remember the road across the pass was quite icy. The Bossart family had come to see us off. Don, the father, was a professor at Iliff. Stephen had become very friendly with Allan, one of the sons. When we drove down the lane at the back of the house where we had done all the loading, Allan ran after the van actually howling to see Stephen go. We found it terribly sad and I can almost still hear Allan. It wasn't nearly as difficult for Stephen as he had a new experience of the trip ahead of him. Mary had quite a time doing the final clean up of the house. Paul and Stephen and I have good memories of that epic journey, stopping at a motel on the western side of the Rockies with one of the biggest dogs we had ever seen; finding out that the truck which was supposed to be governed to a certain speed, in fact was not; playing the pokies in Las Vegas with a limit of five dollars; finding a motel in Los Angeles within easy reach of the freight place where we had to unload. We had arranged to meet Mary and yourself at the airport after we had unloaded, checked the van in and hired a car. I can remember being late, as there were some delays, which was not easy for Mary as your hyperactivity made delays rather difficult. The only car available for hire was a Ford LTD which was huge and amazingly able to fit all our luggage in the boot. It was amazing how much stuff we had with us this, including Stephen's cello and Paul's violin. We can't remember the order of events. We had promised Paul and Stephen one last visit to Disneyland, this time staying in Disneyland hotel. They had been on at least two occasions when we lived in San Diego. On the day we spent going around the various features they were back in the hotel room before us. It seemed it had lost some of its magic. We enjoyed our time back in Pacific Beach, meeting up with people we had known again and were grateful to the Sabatkas, where we stayed. I preached on the Sunday morning which was a great thrill. The memory of getting to San Francisco is rather dim except for the hugeness of the airport and the struggling around with the enormous number of articles we carried with us. This last problem was overcome to some extent when we went to a shop with all sorts of imports from around the world and purchased an African carry bag. We ate at Fisherman's wharf, stayed in a very noisy motel and eventually got on board ship. The passage back was over two weeks and could have been relaxing for Mary and myself but there were a few problems. There was a childminding area functioning in the daytime, but it was absolutely crowded so we could only use the facility if one of us was there as you needed special care. At mealtimes, Paul and Stephen and yourself would eat at the children's time, and then they would look after you while Mary and I would have our meal. It is always difficult adjusting to time zones on a trip like that which meant that you woke up earlier and earlier. We had to devise ways to occupy you. The cabin was out as on the first morning on board ship we had people hammering on the partition walls as they considered we were being a bit noisy. We finished up going up on deck and generally walking around until the pool was open at 6am. The ship called at Honolulu and we visited Pearl Harbor and did some shopping, and also Suva where we managed to meet up with some of the people we had known when we were there. Paul and Stephen had a ball on board ship, making friends with a couple of others of their age and going to movies, some of which, from all accounts were supposed to be restricted.

It was a good moment for Mary and myself when we went through Sydney heads and had the sense of being home again. We were met at the wharf by your Grandma and Grandpa Buckle and your Grandpa Davis who had driven from Brisbane in a car he had purchased with our money, a Holden Kingswood. It was quite a hassle getting through customs as we had acquired a couple of things on the way back but Mary's mother had explained that you were hyperactive so that we received special consideration. Dad had booked us into a motel but I had to fly down to Melbourne to be interviewed by the Council for Christian education in schools. I felt very at home in the interview but didn't hear till the next day after flying back to Sydney that I had been accepted. My father flew back to Brisbane and we followed Mary's mother and Cec. back to Brisbane in our new car. Just as well we had this arrangement as I had to get used to driving on the left-hand side of the road again, and it wasn't easy.

So began a new phase of our lives and it therefore seems a good place to finish off this letter.

Love Dad

Letter 17

*We settle back into Australia. Being appointed to
Frankston High School. Finding a School for Paul
and Stephen and a Centre for Mark to attend.*

Dear Mark,

We'd come to a new phase in our lives. One unknown was
removed when I heard that I'd been accepted as a chaplain
but there were a few openings available and they would decide
which they thought was the most suitable. We would need
to find a school for Paul and Stephen and a suitable facility
for you. All that was put to one side for a time as we drove
up to Brisbane and spent a couple of weeks staying with your
Grandma and Grandpa Buckle and catching up with other
relatives and some old friends. Mary and I were thrilled to be
back home to some of our old haunts and with great excitement
would point out to Paul and Stephen where we lived as we
grew up and went to school but to them at the time it was a
great yawn. It has become of more interest to them as they
have grown older.

We heard that I had been appointed to be chaplain at Frankston
High School and eventually we headed south but had to do
so by way of Sydney to pick up the Star Craft which had gone
into quarantine from the ship to check for any nasty's which
could possibly be brought into the country. The wiring system
wasn't compatible and had to be adapted. Mary and I had only
been to Melbourne once, and that was only briefly before we
were married, and people in Queensland have a rather warped

view of it, feeling that the weather changes too much with the possibility of all the seasons in one day. We arrived in Frankston on a beautiful Melbourne day. Frankston being the gateway to the Mornington Peninsula, is right on Port Phillip Bay. The sun was shining, the Bay looked beautiful and as we ate lunch we were besieged by flocks of seagulls. We were not able to go directly to the house we would be living in, one owned by the Council for Christian education in schools, as it was temporally occupied by an Anglican minister. It had been arranged for us to stay in a rented house on the outskirts of Frankston. Since it was summer we had only packed light clothing. We hadn't heeded Melbourne's reputation and as we ran into a cold snap, froze at night and finished up even putting carpets on the beds until the local Presbyterian minister, Tom Howells who was the chairman of the Frankston chaplaincy committee, provided some extra clothing and bedding. We thought that Paul and Stephen might have trouble moving directly into the state school system and heard of a new Anglican church school which was opening that year, 1975. It was called Woodleigh and was made up of a number of buildings in a bushland setting offering a variety of extracurricular subjects without a heavy emphasis on competitive sport. After a year when I'd had a chance to see the quality of Frankston high School, they transferred into the school and this is where they completed their schooling and spent some good years. It wasn't always easy for them being accepted as they came across as Americans. We moved into the house in Warringa Road and all our stuff came down from Sydney but we had to purchase quite a lot of furniture. The house was ideal for you as it had a large laundry at the back with an enclosed backyard where you could play. Paul and Stephen and I thought we needed another dog to act as protection for Mary, at least that was the rationalisation. Mary loves dogs as much as the rest of us but feared that she would finish up having to feed him all the time and clean up messes in the yard. I believe everyone promised to turn over a new leaf and share in the chores and I seem to recall actually following through. We answered an advertisement and found a dog, a Labrador – Kelpie Cross, whose owner was moving into a unit which didn't allow pets. He was originally from central Europe and had called the dog, Yodi. We kept the name and had found a dog which was well trained and beautifully natured, at least to humans, but couldn't stand other dogs of any type. He stayed with us for 14 years and was a great asset to the family. We were still looking around for a suitable facility for you.

One Sunday I went to a combined church community function at the Frankston football oval and ran into Dick Matthews who we had met when we were on the island of Vanua Levu in Fiji. We greatly enjoyed his company and that of his wife, Nancy and their three children and were glad to renew the relationship. Through Nancy we learned of a private group called Kankama in Mornington, the next township on the Peninsula, which cared for and worked with severely physically and mentally disabled children. You were accepted into the group. There were some 20 who attended regularly. The association with Kankama lasted for the 10 years we were in Frankston and was a very happy one. The aim was to work with each individual to maximise their potential. It was run by a committee with Mary eventually becoming secretary and working tirelessly for its success. There was full government funding for staff with a 4 to one subsidy for equipment. This meant that there was a constant need to raise funds with all sorts of functions and local groups such as Rotary giving support. At first we think you were picked up and brought home in a taxi and later a small bus was acquired. You have never objected to rides in vehicles of any description, so you enjoyed that part of the day, and as the level of care at Kankama was high and loving you seemed to enjoy being there. The last comment indicates a problem we have always had as we looked after you. As you are not able to express yourself fully we are not always sure of how you're feeling. I mentioned earlier the growling you developed to express disapproval, and this does tell us you're not happy with or impatient about something. Many times however this has to do with something which needs to happen whether you like it or not. We have always worked towards your well-being but have to assume that what we are doing is right with you. It is obvious that you understand a great deal of what is said to you. You used to love toast and vegemite and at one stage got to the point of pushing the lever down to operate the toaster. When she was preparing meals Mary would ask you to get the milk and butter from the refrigerator when she was mashing potatoes, in spite of the fact that you have always gagged on mashed potatoes. The best example of your doing something you don't particularly like because it contributes to your overall enjoyment, is to do with horse riding. There have been a couple of times when you have been involved with horse riding for the disabled. You seemed to really enjoy this and it would be wonderful to know what it is that you find enjoyable about it. One would think that it is contact with these beautiful animals but even though we have always had a dog you have never showed a great deal of interest. Perhaps again it is the motion but for whatever reason you do enjoy it. To be able to participate in this activity it is compulsory to wear a helmet but you have always hated having anything on your head and will not keep a hat on. Gradually it seemed that you came to understand that you wouldn't be able to ride a horse unless you wore a helmet. It was reported to us that you actually went and got a helmet and took it to the person concerned to put it on. All those comments came about from my saying that you seemed to enjoy going to Kankama. At first the group met in a house in Mornington but the Management Committee decided to work towards a specially built facility on the outskirts of the town. After a great deal of work this came about and you spent a lot of good time there. Whenever we're down that way and drive past the place we have a good feeling about it, particularly Mary who worked very hard for the organisation.

I think that seems like a good place to finish this letter so will sign off again.

Love Dad

Letter 18

Buying a house in Frankston. Health problems with Mark. Camping experiences. Respite care for Mark. Camping at Wilson's Promontory. Deciding to move back to Brisbane.

Dear Mark,

We had been in Frankston for about six months when we learned that the Council for Christian education in schools was prepared to pay a housing allowance in place of providing a house so that it was possible to purchase our own house and use a housing allowance to pay it off. We began to look around and I got a phone call one day at school to say that Mary had discovered a house in the next street. When I went to look at it, at first glance from outside I wondered what Mary was thinking about. It was about 70 years old and appeared small and boxlike. When I went through the front door I fell in love with it as Mary had done. It had pressed metal ceilings in the hallway and kitchen, tongue and groove linings with the groove running horizontally. It had three bedrooms and a slow combustion stove in the kitchen in addition to a gas stove. There was also a gas heater in the lounge and after our Denver experience we kept the slow combustion stove and the heater going all winter so that the house was very cosy. Paul and Stephen must have shared one-bedroom for a while as Mary and I had one of the bedrooms and you had another. We eventually lined and sealed the garage and Paul used that as his room which gave him a measure of independence. There was a large enclosed backyard so that you had it made, and could race around and pull grass to your hearts content. We have a good feeling about the house and our life there, as I look back and it was home for nine years. It was the first house that Mary and I had owned. Before that we had stayed in houses owned by the church or Iliff School of Theology. My salary didn't really allow us to meet everyday expenses and pay off a house so Mary had a few part-time jobs during our time in Melbourne. She taught remedial Mathematics first at Cleland High in Dandenong and then at Stella Maris College which later became John Paul College, and also worked in the account section of Givonni, a clothing manufacturer.

There are a couple of developments in your life which stand out in my memory. A couple of times while in Melbourne you had a build up of drugs in your system which caused you to become unstable and to spend a lot of time lying down, which was most unusual. At those times we took you to Royal Children's Hospital where they did blood tests and worked out which particular drug had built up and then they tried to find a suitable balance. You were in hospital for about five days on those occasions. Once the buildup subsided you returned to your usual level of activity. With all due respect to yourself, the hospital found you a little hard to handle so you were discharged on one occasion before you had been fully stabilised. On the next occasion this happened, because of the unsatisfactory outcome earlier, Mary refused to bring you home until she was sure the right balance had been established. I think it was only for one extra night but apparently they found you in other vacant beds and outside the ward One of the nurses wondered to Mary how she coped with your level of hyperactivity. The doctor in charge recommended a local Paediatrician, Dr Weldon, as the one to check your drug levels in future. We found him particularly good. He decided to trial a new drug, Epilim, and it was a real breakthrough.

Your hyperactivity was greatly reduced while you remained quite alert.

It was while we were in Frankston that for some reason occasionally a piece of food would lodge in your throat and would partially block the airway. On these occasions we were not able to clear the food ourselves and we had to take you up to the hospital. Your system would generate an amazing amount of thick saliva. It was obviously very uncomfortable and distressing for you. When we moved to Brisbane and a little later you had moved to Ipswich there were a couple of other episodes like this. The last one became really serious as some of the mucus managed to lodge in your lungs causing pneumonia. For the second time in your life you nearly died and at one stage had to be put on oxygen.

Mary and I found a couple of campgrounds on the beach on Westernport Bay at Shoreham and Point Leo where we would go for a weekend or a few days when we had the chance. We were able to take Yodi and loved to roam along the beaches and look out over the water. We were on one such weekend when the message came that my father Vic Davis, your grandfather had died. He had suffered two other heart attacks and I had been up to visit him after one of them. The doctor who was of Scottish background with a heavy accent called home. Stephen answered with his pronounced American accent and they had great trouble understanding one another. Stephen came down to let us know and I flew up to Toowoomba. Dad was 77 when he died. He had worked in a bank from about 16 and retired early at 60 after he had become a bank manager so he could spend more time following his first love, working for the church. His major focus was Lifeline where he pretty well founded Consumer Credit Counselling in Queensland, using his expertise and experience with finances to help people in financial straits. When he died I lost part of my link with the past but still had mum to maintain those links.

We found a couple of places provided respite care for you so that Mary and I could get away occasionally. One place we stayed where you came as well was at Tidal River in Wilsons Promontory National Park. This is a beautiful part of the world which I visited about three times a year, mostly with groups of staff and students from Frankston high School. The greatest part of the park can only be accessed along walking tracks, with four-wheel-drive vehicles banned. I was keen to show Mary one particular bay called sealers Cove. It was about a 10 km walk. Getting there is mostly downhill and you walked extremely well. To get to the campground involved wading across a creek but on this occasion there had been so much rain the creek was running a banker. We decided to eat lunch on the beach and I was determined to light a fire to cook our lunch. For me having a campfire is one of the really attractive parts of camping. The problem was that most of the wood I collected was wet, so that the fire was very reluctant to get established. All this meant that we were rather late setting out to walk back to tidal River. To make matters worse it started to pour. We were equipped with raingear but you hate getting your head wet and screamed rather loudly. Since a large part of the track back was uphill and by now slippery I had to piggy back you for a lot of it. This was no easy task as that stage you would have been 14 or 15. Fortunately I'd taken a torch as darkness caught up with us. It was freezing so by the time we eventually got back to the van it took some hours to thaw out. Quite an adventure you might say.

Towards the end of 1984 after 10 years in Frankston, it seemed to Mary and me that we needed to move back to Brisbane to be closer to our parents who were, of course, ageing. After the initial couple of years of settling into Frankston high School as chaplain the work developed and had been rewarding. I applied for a position with the education department in Queensland as a teacher in the personal development program and was accepted. By this time Paul had moved into Insurance work and had married Karen Barnes whom he had met at Frankston high. Stephen after completing High School had undertaken a few part-time jobs after finding University rather unsatisfying. He followed Paul into Insurance work. I mentioned earlier a trip up to Brisbane with Mary and yourself and to check out a house which we eventually bought. At the beginning of 1985 I went up to Brisbane and stayed with your Grandma Buckle and Cec while I completed a training course in Personal Development. I returned to Melbourne when the house there was sold and the transaction completed. Mary, you and I, with Yodi, our dog headed off to a new phase in our life. Stephen sometimes says that things were a little different with him. Most times children grow up and move away from parents but his parents moved away from him.

This letter has probably blown out a bit but it seemed a good idea to complete the Melbourne experience. In the next letter we'll talk about life in Brisbane.

Love Dad

Letter 19

Moving to house in Aspley, Brisbane. Mark's development.
Finding Respite Care for Mark. An opening for Residential
Care with Intellectually Handicapped Services.

Mary and I have fond memories of our time in Frankston. We enjoyed our house and had added a large patio at the back and had contemplated adding a room at the top of the house from which we would have had a view across Port Phillip Bay. We had planted some more fruit trees in the backyard, the most successful being an apricot which produced glorious fruit. The first project Paul and Stephen and I had undertaken had been to put down a large block of cement with a basketball ring and backboard. Both of them became very interested in basketball and both played for a number of years in top teams with Stephen finishing up in the National basketball league.

The house at Aspley in Brisbane proved very comfortable. It was really on three levels, with the bedrooms of which there were four on one level, the kitchen, dining room and lounge opening out to the front yard on another and on the lowest level, a spare room which I used as a study, the garages and laundry opened out to a fairly large enclosed backyard. There was only the need to put up an extra fence on one side. This meant that you had an area to run around in, although we had to put up some extra wire as you were able to step over the low fence on one side. Your bedroom was at the top of the stairs and had an air conditioner. You adapt very quickly to new places, which certainly had been very helpful to us as we moved around so much. By the time we moved to Brisbane you were 21 so had become a young man, sadly, thanks to your brain damage, you still had the mental age of two-year-old. We still refer to your older brothers as the boys because however old offspring become, they are still to some extent their parent's children but this sort of attitude is magnified with you. Your responses are most times those of a two-year-old and you certainly don't look your age. The brain damage also affected your sexual development. You didn't seem to go through puberty in that there were no "wet dreams" and no desire for masturbation and no apparent attraction to the opposite sex. This is a big slice of life that has been removed from you. It has however been with some relief there has not been the need to make some drastic decisions in regard to your functioning and to seek to modify your behaviour. We have been aware of intellectually handicapped people who have not realised that masturbation is not something to be done in public, which may not be embarrassing for them, but certainly is for those who care for them, and those who may be observers. We have also known parents who have agonised over whether to ensure that their intellectually handicapped off spring are not able to produce children through having a hysterectomy or vasectomy performed. This is something which can only be decided on an individual basis. Some argue that to have these procedures done is to interfere with the rights of the person concerned. My feeling is that if the individual is not able to care for their offspring it is better to remove the possibility of producing them. If a person's disability has a genetic cause there seems to be little point in possibly passing on that defect to another generation. The need for these decisions has been mercifully removed for us, but we do feel for those who have to consider them. In Melbourne you went off to Kankama each weekday but we were unable to find anything equivalent in Brisbane. During the six weeks training time I had for my work in the Personal Development Programme, I had looked at a few places but there were no openings. This meant that Mary was involved with your constant care during the day. We eventually managed to arrange for you to go to Multicap Meadows one day a week and this was extended to 2 days after a while. You were picked up and brought home by taxi. They endeavoured to work with you to explore your potential. The contact with Multicap has continued since that time so that you have been going there for some 30 years. We also managed to get you into respite care at Basil Stafford centre which we weren't happy with, and Mamre, a Catholic run household where we thought the level of care was great. We became associated with the committee of the Uniting Church looking at the future directions of the WR Black home which had cared for severely handicapped children for many years. The main problem was that the residents who had originally been children had become adults and there was no ongoing program to accommodate them. We met an attitude during our involvement which we have come across on a few occasions. Some of the people whose offspring had been in the WR Black home for a good many years were rather fearful of using government facilities and made the comment that they were reluctant to move out of a "Christian environment". Our attitude has always been that one of the chief criteria by which to judge any facility or caring person should be the level of competence shown as well as the ability to care. Christian commitment should lead to the latter but has nothing to do with the former. This is probably the time to make a comment about the great number of people who have cared for you in one way or another over the years. The ones we have most appreciated have been those who have shown genuine concern for your welfare and have had a practical approach to working with people like yourself. We have at times been very frustrated by those who may have a high level of theoretical training through various courses they have undergone whose expectations are unrealistic. The example which stands out most clearly in my mind is our interview with a lady who had just been appointed as a social worker with a community home in which you were living. We had been invited, as had other parents, to meet her and we were keen to do so, but at that stage she hadn't met you and the others in the house. She proceeded to speak about the various programs she was planning to introduce. Amongst these was the intention to take you to do your banking each week. This is something which is completely beyond your capability or interest. You do count up to about 20 but make no connection with anything such as fingers or coins. We thought that this aim was not in touch with reality, although we knew that you would enjoy the trip in the car to get to the bank and the whole outing. I'm not suggesting that there should not be high levels of training to prepare people to be carers, whatever the field, but that there should be a large component of fieldwork.

After about two years at Aspley we had to make one of the most difficult decisions of our lives. We had cared for you at home for 22 years in various places and with many ups and downs as I've mentioned in these letters. We had not been able to find regular day care for you and were offered a place in residential care at Challenor in Ipswich, a centre run by what was then the Intellectually Handicapped Services Division of the Queensland government. We had made contact with a lady whom we had known many years before who had a great deal to do with the program at Challenor, Beth McRobert, and she called one day to tell Mary that there was a place for you. Challenor was a huge institution involved in the care of the intellectually handicapped but the buildings have since become a university as other arrangements have been made for the original residents. When this offer was made a process had been commenced in which the buildings and residents were divided up into self-contained units with about 20 in each. This was an effort to break down the sense of institutionalisation. Also at this time, your grandmother, my mother had what appeared to be a minor stroke causing her to be very disoriented and she had to spend time in hospital. She was 87 at the time and it was obvious that she would not be able to live by herself any longer. There was some thought that she may have to come to live with us which would have been an incredible burden, particularly for Mary. As it turned out there was one place left in a new development at the Garden Settlement in Toowoomba called Minna Murra and Mum moved in there.

Mary and I had decided that, if at all possible, we would find a place where you could be cared for before we became too old to do so adequately. We had been aware of a number of families with severely handicapped people who were being cared for by elderly parents and the question had to be asked what would happen when the parents died? Given that we have no idea how long we will live or how healthy we will be in the future, we needed to make suitable arrangements while we could still keep a check on them. We were conscious also that if anything did happen to us the responsibility for your care would fall on Paul and Stephen and their wives and we didn't want them to be faced with that situation. When you became brain damaged through meningitis, the course of your natural development changed as I've explained in these letters and you therefore needed a great deal more care and attention than would normally have been the case. This had an enormous effect on the total family including Paul and Stephen. Again, I've commented on this in other letters. I consider that the effects have been mainly positive but Mary and I were convinced that their lives had been sufficiently affected and that they needed to be able to establish their own families without direct concern for your care. All that is preliminary to saying that we decided to accept a place for you at Challenor. I said a little earlier that this was one of the most difficult decisions of our lives and it was indeed. Were we doing the right thing by you? Were we shirking our ongoing responsibility? I can remember looking out the window one afternoon as you ran round the backyard of the house at Aspley and just bursting into tears as I wondered if we had made the right decision. You see we had no way of talking it over with you and no way of knowing how you would feel about it. I can't remember the actual occasion when we first took you and your things to Challenor. I can remember the part of the complex where you lived. Every effort had been made to make it comfortable and there was a large enclosed grassy area so that you would not feel too confined. I think that is enough for one letter so I will finish off and write again.

Love Dad

Letter 20

*More about Challenor. Moving into separate
housing. Concluding letters.*

Dear Mark,

As time has gone on we have been convinced that we made the right decision. When we accepted your placement at Challenor you became mostly the responsibility of the state. We are still consulted about decisions which need to be made to do with your healthcare and we are kept informed about any change in arrangements such as housing. The same will still apply with your next of kin when we are no longer living. We have made weekly contact with you over the years, usually taking you for a drive and for a meal somewhere, and will continue to do so as long as we are able. We feel our decision was for the best for a number of reasons. First of all, we have been happy with the level of care you have received. Because of the extent of your handicap, you will always need 24-hour care and this has been provided from our point of view with your well-being in mind. While I guess never losing the sense of loss we felt when you became brain damaged through meningitis, we do have a sense of ease, in that we know you will be well cared for no matter what happens to us. It meant that later Mary and I were able to apply for positions advertised at Somerville House, a Uniting and Presbyterian Church Girl's school in South Brisbane. Mary became the Senior Mistress of the Boarding School, a position she held for five years, and I became the Chaplain, a role I filled for 11 years until my retirement. I mentioned in a much earlier letter that your disability had an effect on the whole family but on your mother in particular. In a sense you became her major concern even though she by no means neglected the rest of the family. In her work at Somerville she was able to call into play her background in teaching, work with young people through the church, bookkeeping and her general skills in organisation. This combined with real concern for the well-being of the girls in the boarding school and her sense of responsibility meant that the job was handled extremely well and prospered.

While your Grandma Davis was alive you had a particularly long drive once a fortnight as we would pick you up and drive up to Toowoomba to see her. By seeing you every week we have indicated our ongoing concern and can note the level of care you are receiving. We have been very happy with the level of care you have received over the years and have a lot of respect for those who work in this situation. Certainly they are responsible for just their shift as opposed to the 24-hour care provided by a family but they are looking after five severely intellectually handicapped people. We are left in no doubt about your feelings when we come to pick you up each week. The check is always made with your house that it is all right to pick you up at whatever time we have in mind. They tell us, that, when they tell you that we are coming and get you ready, you keep saying Mum and Dad until we arrive. At times you seem to have learned the sound of the car so that when you have heard it come running out to greet us. I have to say we're never sure whether the excitement is over seeing us personally or the association with the ride in the car or the treats we always give you on a plate we keep in the car. Fortunately you always go back into the house happily when we take you back.

You have had a number of places of abode since moving into Challenor. The first was to a large house in the community with nine other severely intellectually handicapped people. When the suggestion was made that you moved to this house we readily agreed as we were keen to have you in a situation which is as close as possible to being in a household. This worked out well. When possible houses are being considered as places of residence for people like yourself, the neighbours are always consulted. Some people object because, in most cases, they are completely unfamiliar with the reactions of those who are intellectually handicapped. Their objections are often brought about by fear of the unknown and thought of possible harm to themselves, their children or their property. I'm not sure what method is used in the consultation process but I'm sure possible neighbours are assured there would be no attempt to place people who would be harmful to the community and that there would be 24 hour care. That first household was later divided into two groups of five. Since then you have mostly lived with your original four housemates in four different houses. Over the years there have been changes brought about by death or illness. At the time of writing there is only one person of the original 10 who lives in the house with you. The house you live in now will hopefully be your permanent home. It was specially built with government funds which are being repaid through contributions taken from the invalid pensions of the five of you. Those pensions also pay ongoing costs such as food and clothing. Anything in excess of these amounts is put into your own savings account.

Well son, this will probably be the last letter for a while. We've reached the present. Your mum and I retired to our dream home, the first one we've built to our own plan drawn up with the aid of an architect, at the beginning of 1998. We looked over Moreton Bay to Russell and Stradbroke Islands. Our land on Lamb Island sloped down to a pebbly beach. On one occasion you came down with your four housemates and two carers to have the day on the island which went well. At the end of 2003 we put the house on the market and moved into an independent living unit in a retirement complex in Ipswich about five minutes from where you live.

It has been good to write these letters. It's almost unbelievable the way things worked out over the years. As I've said on a few occasions, it is indeed like a saga when you consider where we have lived. We earnestly wish that you had never contacted meningitis but tragically it happened, and we have learned to cope – fortunately, mostly successfully, but many times it hasn't been easy. Life is a learning experience from beginning to end and I have to say there have been some steep learning curves as we have endeavoured to function as a family. It is in order to consider the future. Of course no one knows for sure but apart from unforeseen circumstances, this is how I see it. You should be cared for in your current situation for the rest of your life. Mary and I will keep in touch as long as we are around and able. Your two older brothers, Paul and Stephen have said that they will always check on your welfare. They have both considered looking for places where you could be cared for closer to them but it is very difficult to get someone like yourself into the caring system of a different state and why move you from a favourable situation. A great indication of the ongoing care and affection that your brothers have for you was when Paul and his wife Annette named their fourth son after you. His name is Gabriel Mark. All that is left is to wish you Godspeed.

Love Dad

Post Script

This postscript is written in 2017 over 12 years since "Letters to Mark" was self published. The whole book has been revised but I thought it good to be completely up to date with Mark's current situation. He still lives in Blackstone in the purpose-built complex as described in the last letter. Mark is now 53 so he has defied the predictions made when he first got meningitis that he wouldn't live beyond his teenage years. He and his fellow residents are looked after around the clock. We still pick him up once a week and take him for a drive and mostly bring him home for lunch. We have reduced the time we spend with him because if he should have a seizure we no longer have the strength to give him much help. Recently his oldest brother, Paul who now lives in Ourimbah on the Central Coast of New South Wales came for a brief visit. We were thrilled that Mark knew him even though it's over two years since they saw one another. Mark still goes to Multicap twice a week. Conveniently there is now a branch here in Ipswich. He is showing signs of ageing as, of course, are his parents. He seems to be getting arthritis which is understandable as Mary has some osteoarthritis as did her mother and Noel has degenerative arthritis.

We have been keeping close watch on the introduction of the Disability Insurance Scheme. We consider it a great innovation which should ensure that no disabled person misses out on support or full care. We want to try and ensure that Mark continues to receive at least the level of care he has been receiving. As I write this it seems that he will be well cared for. Since we have the right to choose his carers we will opt for a continuation of the present arrangement.

Appendix 1

Epilepsy

In letter 2 it is mentioned that Mary brought Mark home to Nasavusavu from Suva and that Mark started to have seizures which we had never experienced before but came to recognise and to some extent understand over the years which followed. I think it makes sense to write this appendix about epilepsy or seizures as we came to understand them. This is not an attempt to give a medical summary as this is far from my area of expertise but dealing with seizures did become a part of our life with Mark.

Epilepsy comes about when some part of the brain is damaged perhaps through the birth process, disease affecting the brain, as with Mark or through accident. Electrical activity occurs in the brain in connection with thought, memory or mobility. When there is a seizure it has been brought about by as it were, a short circuit in the process and a surge of electrical activity. It is this which causes the reactions mentioned in the second letter, the spasms, the rolling eyes, the occasional blanking out.

When Mark became mobile a couple of years later and then really for the rest of his life, the seizures became far more noticeable. Depending on the part of the brain which is damaged, the type of seizures may vary. In Mark's case it was obvious that sensations occurred which let him know a seizure was about to occur. He would make a grunting sound which would warn us that we needed to hold him loosely as the seizure would make him want to run. However he was not entirely conscious of where he was running. In a house we would direct him to a passage way so that he could run up and down. So we would hold him loosely until the seizure started to pass and then allow him to run. I guess we thought that to do so would help him deal with the seizure more quickly. He would put his hands up and crash into the wall at each end of the passage way.

For whatever reason Mark's seizures have changed in their nature. In later years the seizures have become more of the dropping variety which I had observed in others with epilepsy. There are spasms. It is a matter of making sure that the person having the seizure does not harm themselves.

There are many drugs which help to control seizures and Mark has been prescribed a number over the years. Doctors prescribe these drugs in a dosage they deem appropriate but the drug or the dosage may not be appropriate to various individuals. It is a matter of trial and error. This really has been the story of Mark's life from the time he was affected by meningitis. Combined with epilepsy has been hyperactivity which can also be controlled by appropriate drugs. Over a period time drugs can build up in the system and cause someone to function at a lower level than should be possible. Getting the right balance of drugs is a necessity, seeking control of epilepsy and/ or hyperactivity while allowing the individual to have maximal functioning. In the course of the letters the hyperactivity which may come with brain damage is described. It far transcends the energetic behaviour of an unaffected child.

Over the years we learnt that a number of factors would make it more likely Mark would have seizures. We could not afford to let him become too hot or cold as this could bring on seizure activity The part of the brain which helps control reaction to temperature change had been damaged by the meningitis.

Because of the profound brain damage which Mark sustained through meningitis he has not been able to be involved in sheltered workshops or anything approaching them. There are a number of people with epilepsy who are not handicapped in any other way who are able to be involved in the work place and community activities. They are often nervous about doing so because of the unfamiliarity with epilepsy on the part of most. There has over the years been a growth in understanding of the condition and it can be mostly controlled by various drugs. Those who have not witnessed seizure activity find it rather frightening. As I indicated earlier the most important thing to be done is to ensure there is nothing in the person's environs to cause them harm and to be watchful till the spasm has passed. They will most often be very tired once the seizure has finished.

Appendix 2

The Doman Delacato Method

The main reason for going to America was to access the Doman Delacato method with the hope that Mark would benefit. It makes sense to include some information about this program.

I have to say that there has always been a question mark over the method by some in the medical field. Not long before we left Fiji, Dr Howard Clinebell who was the Professor of Clinical Pastoral Education at Claremont in Southern California, visited Suva and I had the opportunity to hear him speak. I asked him about the Doman Delacato Method. He was by no means encouraging stating that it wasn't widely accepted. We were well advanced in our arrangements and our hopes were high, so we went ahead.

In a review on the "net" the comment is made, "the Doman Delacato Method" has helped many people, adults and children and even babies lead a fuller and more meaningful life."

The method was developed between 1955 and 1964 for "brain injured" children. It was developed by Glenn Doman, a physical therapist, and Carl Delacato, an educational psychologist. They drew on the theories of Dr Temple Fay who at that time was head of the Department of Neurosurgery at Temple University Medical School and President of the Philadelphia Neurological Society. Doman and Delacato used Dr. Fay's theory that human brains develop in stages similar to the "tree of evolution" from a fishlike state at conception, up through a reptilian phase, then up to mamalian, and finally to human. This theory of brain development is outdated and was discarded entirely by the 1980s. The method is also developed from the idea of neuro plasticity, which basically states that the brain has an inherent ability to grow both functionally and anatomically. Healthy portions of the brain can pick up on functions of damaged portions. I feel that the more recent work on the plasticity of the brain by Dr Norman Doidge as put forward in his book "The Brain That Changes Itself" adds credence to the "Method". What the brain seems to do with damaged areas is, in effect, reroute as many functions as possible. People who have had brain injury affecting touch e.g. have with constant stimulation of the body rerouted their sensory abilities to mirroring sections of the brain.

The Doman-Delacato Method uses techniques such as patterning, crawling, creeping, expressive activities, amongst others (there is more about the various activities in Letter 8) The first step, patterning, means to move the head, arms, legs in rhythmical repetitive patterns. Crawling means to help the child do forward motions with the abdomen in contact with the floor, while creeping means to do forward motion with the abdomen off the floor. It does seem to be a turnaround in terminology, but these are specific definitions used for this method. "Expressive activities" refers to play activities like the picking up of objects.

The patterning program needs the involvement of five people, one at the head, one on each side of the body as a pattern is followed, the head being turned towards the right side as the arm and leg on that side are moved up. The same thing then happens on the left side. This is accompanied by counting or in our case nursery rhymes to establish a rhythm. The result has been that Mark loves to count even though he doesn't relate the numbers with any particular objects. He also has a good repertoire of nursery rhymes which he likes to recite with help.

The expressive activities require the involvement of at least one dedicated person. In Mark's case this was Mary who was truly dedicated.

The review article makes a telling statement after referring to various clinical studies on the method. "Children who receive this much attention will almost always show increased intellectual function over those that don't. We know that children who get high amounts of healthy interaction are better adjusted, better developed and smarter than children who get less or no healthy interaction."

After three years of faithful adherence to the program we had to move on. While we have to say there didn't seem to be any intellectual improvement in Mark's functioning the program had enormous positive effects in his socialisation. He had positive contact with a number of caring, accepting people.

Appendix 3

Socialisation

Whenever parents give birth to a child and a new individual enters the world it is, in the normal course of events, a joyous occasion. There is promise and no one really knows at that stage the actual potential of that new individual. Parents have a huge responsibility to seek to ensure that their child grows up to take a positive, worthwhile place in society. There is possibly no way of calculating the amount of writing and discussion over the centuries to do with the source of human characteristics, how much is innate and how much comes from the socialisation process mainly from parents, particularly in the early years.

When our first son was born as I held him for the first time part of my thinking was to do with whether I was really up to the task of caring for and guiding him. It seems that every child seeks as they grow up to explore the boundaries of acceptable behaviour as they hopefully realise that the needs of others should be considered. A vital realisation when one is considering fitting into society is that one can't always expect to get one's own way.

Paul, our first child, seemed to be independent almost from the time he emerged into the world. We were very concerned when he hadn't spoken much even up to his second birthday. When he did really start talking he spoke in sentences and we became convinced that in his own small mind he had decided baby talk was not for him. We were determined that our children would behave the way we desired and not cause unnecessary disruption to others. I have a distinct memory of Paul who was wearing little boots to help correct flat feet lying on the floor and kicking his little boots as he threw a tantrum. At the time I smacked him and he did stop. I stress I didn't beat him I smacked him on the legs. As I look back I realise it would probably have been just as effective to ignore him. This is an example of our socialisation process with Paul. We used smacking when he had been asked to carry out some specific task or behave in a certain manner but did not follow through. Happily the need for this receded as he got older. I had decided I would not use smacking as discipline beyond the age of seven.

I can't recall ever smacking Stephen our second son. He occasionally persisted in not following through on something he was asked to do or misbehaved but a spoken reprimand was sufficient.

Mark was different again. Since he suffered two thirds brain damage he didn't understand a lot of what was said to him and it was impossible to explain to him what we wanted. His reaction to pain was also different to the average person. In one of the letters I referred to the fact that Mary found him one day lying across the door of the oven without any sign of discomfort. In other words smacking did not work as a way of deterring unacceptable behaviour. He had, however, been born into society and would have to be involved with people so the socialisation process was just as important for him to ease that involvement.

When Mary took Mark to see Dr Spitz who himself was bringing up an intellectually disabled child who someone had just left with him and his wife he spoke of the fact that they had resorted to using a dog prod as a way of dealing with unacceptable behaviour. We had never heard of such a thing. It is about a foot long and is operated with batteries and when a button is pressed emits a mild charge. We ordered one through the mail. I picked it up at the post office and tried it on myself on the way home. It does cause quite a sharp pain when the button is pressed. It also makes a buzzing noise at that time. Fortunately we only had to use it once on Mark, touching him on one of his legs. If we were trying to stop some unacceptable behaviour, after that we only had to push the button to cause the buzzing sound and say, "do you want the stick Mark?" We were most reluctant to do this as it seems so radical but we feel it saved our sanity. We had not been able to find a way to stop him pulling drawers in an out and dragging out the contents, whatever they might be, or taking things off shelves in stores etc, etc. The resultant better behaviour meant that he was able to fit more readily into social environments.

It will not be surprising to most that we debated including the information about this aspect of our care of Mark particularly in the current atmosphere to do with smacking as a way of disciplining children. We did so for the sake of total honesty and because, in general, Mark is able to fit socially into various environments.

We realise that such treatment could readily lend itself to physical abuse. Also such treatment should most certainly be a last resort.

Printed in the United States
By Bookmasters